DECISIVE
JUDO

Written and illustrated

by

DES MARWOOD

Decisive Judo
Published in 1998 by
Ippon Books,
36 Highcroft,
North Hill,
N6 4RD

ISBN 1874572 41 0

First published by A & C Black (Publishers) Ltd 1992 under the title
Critical Judo.

ABOUT THE AUTHOR

Des Marwood's first experience of judo was at the London Judo
Society's Vauxhall *dojo* back in the 1950s. Pressure of media work on
national newspapers as a reporter, feature writer, sports cartoonist,
illustrator, designer, executive and international publisher prohibited
him from taking the sport seriously until he found himself being lured
back to a *dojo* ten years later. He has, for a number of years, run the
Yoshinkwai Judo Club in London.

Acknowledgement

My gratitude is expressed to Brian Caffary (5th Dan) for the patient help
and guidance he gave whenever I sought his advice on matters
concerned with the preparation of this book.

Des Marwood.

Printed and bound in Great Britain by
Redwood Books, Trowbridge, Wiltshire

CONTENTS

isive Judo was born from the thought I gave to
ments heard from so many judoka who were in
ch of a reference book which showed clearly just
techniques should be performed.

hilst no one believes seriously that judo, or any
r form of athleticism, may be learned solely from
ook, it is undeniably a look-learn-and-do-by-
nple sporting activity. So, I thought a book which
e down techniques graphically into separate
uences with caption commentaries would surely
ide such a reference and would at least stimulate
tal rehearsals. I hope **Decisive Judo** does just
and that with the help of my specially created
graph illustrations it will provide a useful
dement to any judoka's training programme.

any actions made in judo are performed at speed
full commitment. However, there are certain
al points, or stages, in many attacks when tori,
ever momentarily, is weak and vulnerable to
ter attack. Conversely, he may be ideally
ioned to carry on into alternative or combination
w-through techniques, should a first attack have
d. Such points, or stages, are highlighted and
nded in the critical path analysis style of the
graph illustrations.

arning to perfect a single technique is
enging enough to any student and I have no
to encourage a beginner to leap-frog into
nced combinations before basics have been
tered. That is why **Decisive Judo** is not
tionally a book of counter or combination
niques. The inclusion of simple examples of
e of these within the judographs is intended to
ulate an early awareness, or to provide a
nder, of the benefits of a style of judo which is
flowing and full of objective movement.

mittedly, each mainstream technique must be
nt and learned independently. It is when these
idual techniques begin to be put into practice by
student in either randori (practice) or shiai

(contest) combat situations that they too often
become wasteful of energy. A player who turns in to
execute a nage-waza (throwing technique) or rolls
over to apply katame-waza (groundwork technique)
and fails to achieve either, too often locks into an
energy-wasting and non-scientific struggle before
turning or rolling out again with absolutely no
advantage having been achieved.

The effective and objective action is to transform a
failed attack into a new offensive, launching into a
different technique which is directed along the same
line of energy force as that of the attacker's original
momentum, or transferring it to move in the direction
of the reverse action of the defender's resistance.

Whichever, this principle re-uses invested energy. It
keeps the action 'rolling', with none of the stop-go
style of judo demonstrated by so many kyu grades.
Judo becomes fluid and flowing and that makes for
good judo.

Whilst every effort has been made to ensure the
accuracy of the judograph demonstrations,
remember that the manner of execution of some
elements of some techniques depends upon
personal interpretation or preferences. So, don't fall
out with your sensei if his methods differ from some
of those displayed in judographs.

Generally, all judographs show right-handed
techniques being performed. Occasionally, for the
purposes of a clearer demonstration, left-handed
techniques are shown. In any case, practise all your
techniques from both sides. For the purpose of clarity
in combat situations, tori's judogi (judo suit) is tinted
and uke's is left white in all the illustrations.

Throughout the book, 'he' is the composite gender,
referring not only to the male judoka but also to the
many females, young and not-so-young, who
participate, enjoy and help bring honour and
recognition to the sport of judo.

Des Marwood

INTRODUCTION

of the books in the Ippon Books catalogue are
en by leading figures in judo who are known for
cular techniques and illustrated by photographs
n by experienced specialist photographers.

t drawings can also show very clearly the details
technique, the directions of pull and push - even
whole nature and feel of a throw or a hold. The
em is finding an artist who is not just copying a
ograph, but who truly understands what judo is
about.

his sense, Des Marwood has been able to make
articular contribution to judo literature with his

Decisive Judo, for he is both an accomplished
illustrator and an active judo teacher with a sound,
classical understanding of judo itself.

This book, originally published under the title
Critical Judo, is now back in print, in the Ippon
catalogue. It is admirably direct and simple in its
format, a useful introduction to the subject as a
whole.

Nicolas Soames
Ippon Books

BACKGROUND TO JUDO

The common origin of all forms of unarmed combat must be buried in the deep mists of time, when people first fought tooth and nail against each other for a morsel of food on the floor of a cave. Later, as century rolled over century and millennium covered millennium, the practice of hand-to-hand fighting as a means of either establishing physical superiority or providing protection became more disciplined and structured as special proven techniques were developed.

Ancient civilisations organised their combat sports, such as fist-fighting and wrestling, and these were often the basis from which more militaristic martial arts evolved for use by warriors in battle. Or, the reverse may have happened and the sports reflected in a competitive manner a version of techniques used in warfare.

Whatever was the case, it is perhaps surprising that even today, in an age of awesome nuclear weaponry, the troops of all nations are still trained in the ancient skills of unarmed combat!

Almost all martial arts disciplines are of oriental origin. *Ju-jutsu* (or *ju-jitsu* as it has now become) was originally the generic name in Japan during the sixteenth and seventeenth centuries for a variety of systems by which opponents fought each other with little or no weapon support. This fighting discipline employed the use of hand-strikes, kicks and a variety of grappling and throwing techniques, as well as *atemi*, which is the aiming of blows at vital points of an opponent's body. They were all amongst the armoury of the Samurai warrior.

Towards the latter part of the nineteenth century, there were very many different *ryu* (schools) of *ju-jutsu* being taught throughout Japan and one student of this martial art form, or discipline, was a young man by the name of Jigoro Kano.

JIGORO KANO

Kano was born in 1860 and, while pursuing a academic career at Tokyo University, he foun time to examine in depth the teaching principle of some of the great *ju-jutsu* Masters of the da He was perplexed by the fact that, while they eac taught a range of techniques, none had seemed have seized upon a single or common princip which might be applied to all. He came to th conclusion that the most effective principle gov erning the whole field of striking and throwin in all or any direction should be 'the highest o most efficient use of mental as well as physic energy, directed to the accomplishment of certain definite purpose or aim.'

He applied this principle to his study of all *j jutsu* techniques, focusing on those aspec which concerned the disturbance of points balance of the defender to the benefit of th attacker being able to employ minimum energ for maximum results. He deleted any technique with lethal elements or which were too dangerou for use in open competition. Some he modifie others he created anew, but all were based upo *ju-jutsu* principles.

Gradually, Professor Kano gathered technique around what he eventually called his 'Principle Maximum Efficiency'. He incorporated these in 'Kodokan Judo', *Kodokan* meaning 'a school f studying the way'. In a Japanese Tourist boa booklet published during the 1930s Profess Kano proclaimed:

Ju-do and *ju-jutsu* are [each] composed of two words, meaning 'gentle' or 'to give way', *jutsu*, 'art' or 'practic and *do*, 'way' or 'principle'. Thus, *ju-do* means the w of gentleness or of first giving way in order ultimately gain the victory, while *ju-jutsu* means the art and pra tice of judo...

1 One thing that can happen when an attack fails is shown above when *tori* (the attacker) turns in to execute *tai-o-toshi*.

2 *Uke* (defender) takes immediate advantage of *tori*'s hesitancy and steps forwards to take *tori* off balance.

1 Another critical point of attack during which *tori* is vulnerable to a counter is when, having turned in to execute, for instance, an *uchi-mata*...

2 ...he is unable to complete the technique. As he begins to turn out, *uke* takes advantage of his opponent's transfer of energy direction...

3 ..by extending his leg as a prop, dropping to the rear left corner (see page 15 for explanation of 'corners') and using *tori*'s established momentum to help throw him backwards onto the mat.

f I explain *ju-jutsu* as the art and practice of the most cient use of mental and physical energy, and *ju-do* as way or principle, we can for the first time say that we e arrived at the true definition of these words.

Meanwhile, young Kano had pursued his study literature, politics and political economy to duate from Tokyo University in 1881. One year er, at the age of twenty-three, he had com- ted the structure of what he called the Kodokan hool for Judo and a memorial stone in the Bud- st Temple Eisojhi remains to commemorate e event. Today's multi-storeyed Kodokan Inter- tional Judo Centre in the Bunkyo Ward of kyo comprises several dojos, changing and rest oms, overnight accommodation, conference ls and exhibition facilities, administration offi- s and a Judo Hall of Fame.

Perhaps a more splendid monument to the cre- ve and pioneering work of Professor Jigoro no has been the manner in which *judo* has spread in popularity throughout the world, establishing a global group able to meet, practise and communicate through the universal language of *judo*.

Apart from pursuing an academic career, Professor Kano was for ever championing the cause of his beloved *judo* and in 1919 became his country's first representative to sit on the International Olympic Committee. Two years later, he became the first President of the newly-founded Japanese Amateur Sports Association. He continued to travel the world, promoting the interests of Japanese sport and of *judo* in particular. Sadly, it was whilst returning home from a 1938 meeting of the IOC in Cairo that Professor Kano died on board ship and never experienced the triumph of *judo* making its debut as an Olympic event at the 1964 Tokyo Games. *Judo* was dropped from the 1968 Mexico Olympic Games, but was restored for Munich in 1972.

GETTING STARTED

Judo is practised by boys and girls of all ages and by people from all walks of life in many venues throughout the world every day or evening of any week of the year. They abide by identical rules and codes of conduct, wear similar *judogi* (outfits), and all communicate their sport in a common language.

Premises may differ widely, ranging from a luxuriously equipped multi-sports complex or custom-built building to a humble community hall or large wooden outbuilding. During the time it is used for *judo*, the space upon which the mat is laid becomes a *dojo*, demanding respect regardless of situation or surroundings. It becomes the centre of every *judoka*'s life and disciplines.

Many players start by joining one of the many excellent evening institute or leisure centre introductory courses, but nothing can beat the atmosphere of good club *judo*. There, a beginner can not only enjoy instruction and practice with a varied and dedicated level of experienced players, but he can savour the changing room chat, the exchange of anecdotes, the dropping of a few great names, and the glimpse of what *judo*'s all about.

If you are looking for a club, you must first choose the *right* one in your area. Make sure it belongs to an established organisation and that membership provides insurance cover (accidents do happen, sometimes, so it's better to be safe than sorry).

Decide which club suits your own needs. Is it too much of a 'contest' club? Is the instructor properly licensed and qualified to teach? Is it a mixed club? Where are grading examinations held? To which major organisation or controlling body is the club affiliated? Are there children's classes (families may like to join together)? Maybe check facts fully with the national governing body.

Anyone taking up *judo* should be reasonably fit, though it is recommended that a 'mature' beginner especially, and in particular anyone who hasn't indulged in regular physical exercise for some time, should first have a medical check-up. In any case, always tell your instructor before going onto the mat if you suffer from a complaint such as asthma, diabetes or epilepsy – or, in fact, anything of even a temporary nature that's likely to affect your standard of fitness. Discuss how he might keep a special eye on you.

Deafness presents no problem, providing those who are responsible for control of the mat are made aware of the player's condition before he goes onto it.

Youngsters are usually accepted into clubs as Primary Grades from the age of six years. They are Juniors from the age of ten to sixteen years. Afterwards, they become classed as Senior Grades, though there is some provision for them to compete in tournaments in special Espoir categories until their physique matures around the age of nineteen. On average, players reach the maximum level of performance in their mid-twenties. They probably retain it for some ten years although the technical quality of their *judo* may continue to mature after that, providing they remain in regular practice.

Beyond the mid-forties there comes a natural decline in a player's speed, stamina, agility and degree of suppleness. However, with continued training a player's actual skill should always remain or even improve, permitting the older player to practise with and pass on his knowledge to another generation.

In this manner, *judo* may become as much of a lifetime involvement as any might wish to make it. There is a dearth of candidates to qualify as timekeepers, recorders, referees, coaches and all manner of executives concerned wtih the infrastructure of a wonderful sport.

BELTS

The standard of a senior player is indicated by the colour of the belt worn while progressing through the *kyu* (student) grades: White Belt (6th *kyu*), Yellow (5th *kyu*), Orange (4th *kyu*), Green (3rd *kyu*), Blue (2nd *kyu*), and Brown (1st *kyu*). Beyond that comes progress into the Black Belt *dan* grades.

Students qualify for progress at periodic grading examinations, but there is some variance between what each parent Association may require of a member in relation to any particular stage. Differing degrees of importance are placed upon a student's performance of syllabus techniques, contest ability or knowledge of *kata* (see page 128).

Junior players are similarly examined, their progress being recognised not only by the wearing of coloured belts, but also by the fixing of them of differently coloured bands or *mons*.

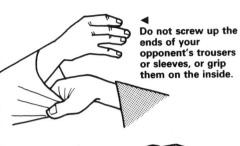

◄ Do not screw up the ends of your opponent's trousers or sleeves, or grip them on the inside.

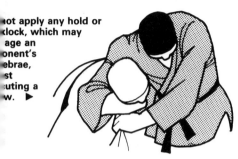

...ot apply any hold or ...lock, which may ...age an ...onent's ...ebrae, ...st ...uting a ...w. ►

Some methods of grappling with or throwing an opponent can be dangerous and are not within the true spirit of *judo*. They are therefore regarded as 'prohibited acts'.

Most 'prohibited acts' are universal throughout *judo*, but it's advisable to ask for a set of rules pertaining to the controlling body of any club you join or to any tournament you enter. That way, you may be absolutely sure of the specific rules under which you are expected to perform.

An outstanding difference between one authority and another, for instance, exists in junior *judo*. The British Judo Council teaches and permits youngsters to use armlocks and strangles, while the British Judo Association forbids this until players reach some age of maturity at which the skeletal structure may be considered to have become properly formed.

Further prohibited acts and rules apply more specifically to contest *judo* situations, so it's advisable to ask your *sensei* for a full set of the rules of your club's governing body. Meanwhile, some other things which you must *not* do are illustrated on this page.

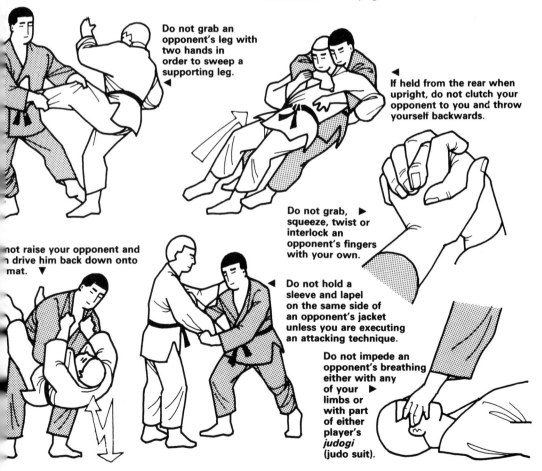

Do not grab an opponent's leg with two hands in order to sweep a supporting leg. ◄

◄ If held from the rear when upright, do not clutch your opponent to you and throw yourself backwards.

Do not grab, ► squeeze, twist or interlock an opponent's fingers with your own.

...not raise your opponent and ...n drive him back down onto ...mat. ▼

◄ Do not hold a sleeve and lapel on the same side of an opponent's jacket unless you are executing an attacking technique.

Do not impede an opponent's breathing either with any of your ► limbs or with part of either player's *judogi* (judo suit).

ETIQUETTE AND DISCIPLINE

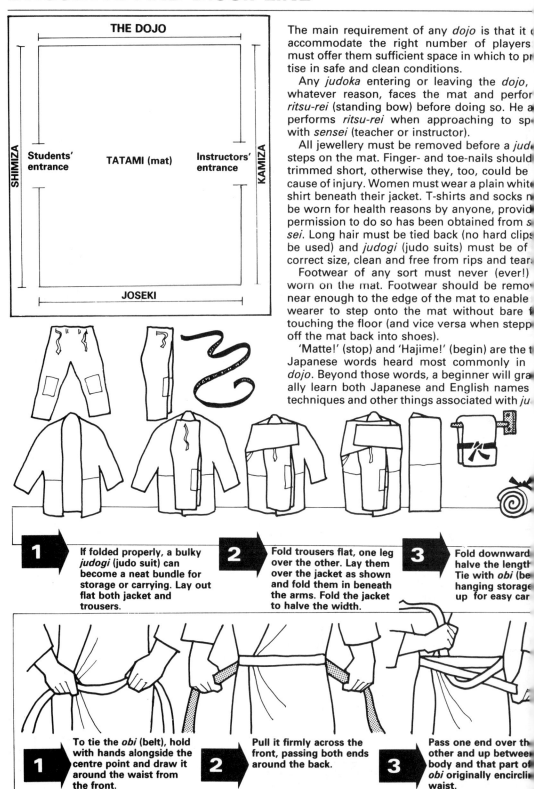

THE DOJO

SHIMIZA

Students' entrance

TATAMI (mat)

Instructors' entrance

KAMIZA

JOSEKI

The main requirement of any *dojo* is that it c accommodate the right number of players must offer them sufficient space in which to pr tise in safe and clean conditions.

Any *judoka* entering or leaving the *dojo*, whatever reason, faces the mat and perfor *ritsu-rei* (standing bow) before doing so. He a performs *ritsu-rei* when approaching to sp with *sensei* (teacher or instructor).

All jewellery must be removed before a *jud* steps on the mat. Finger- and toe-nails should trimmed short, otherwise they, too, could be cause of injury. Women must wear a plain whit shirt beneath their jacket. T-shirts and socks n be worn for health reasons by anyone, provid permission to do so has been obtained from s *sei*. Long hair must be tied back (no hard clip be used) and *judogi* (judo suits) must be of correct size, clean and free from rips and tear

Footwear of any sort must never (ever!) worn on the mat. Footwear should be remo near enough to the edge of the mat to enable wearer to step onto the mat without bare f touching the floor (and vice versa when stepp off the mat back into shoes).

'Matte!' (stop) and 'Hajime!' (begin) are the t Japanese words heard most commonly in dojo. Beyond those words, a beginner will gra ally learn both Japanese and English names techniques and other things associated with *ju*

1 If folded properly, a bulky *judogi* (judo suit) can become a neat bundle for storage or carrying. Lay out flat both jacket and trousers.

2 Fold trousers flat, one leg over the other. Lay them over the jacket as shown and fold them in beneath the arms. Fold the jacket to halve the width.

3 Fold downward halve the length Tie with *obi* (be hanging storage up for easy car

1 To tie the *obi* (belt), hold with hands alongside the centre point and draw it around the waist from the front.

2 Pull it firmly across the front, passing both ends around the back.

3 Pass one end over th other and up betwee body and that part of *obi* originally encircli waist.

1	**2**	**3**	**4**	**5**	**6**

o drop from tanding into a-rei (kneeling ow)...

...always drop onto the left knee, hand on right knee.

Then drop onto both knees, toes turned under.

Sink into *seiza* (kneeling-sit) with hands on your thighs ...

...before sliding hands down thighs and flat onto the mat ...

...with your head toward hands. Pause briefly and then rise again.

RITSU-REI standing bow
To perform *ritsu-rei* (standing bow) from a standing posture with feet together, simply tilt your upper body forwards.

HANDS
When in *seiza*, male players place their hands flat on their upper thighs, with their fingers pointing inwards. Female players place flat hands on their thighs, but with their fingers pointing downwards.

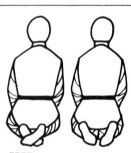

FEET
Many regard it as wrong to cross the feet in *seiza*, preferring them to be separated as shown on the right.

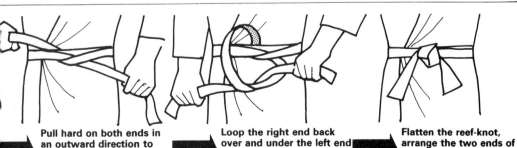

4 Pull hard on both ends in an outward direction to ensure the *obi* is fitting tightly and firmly around the body.

5 Loop the right end back over and under the left end and pull both ends outwards to form a reef-knot.

6 Flatten the reef-knot, arrange the two ends of the *obi* neatly, adjust the jacket, and be ready for action.

BALANCE AND MOVEMENT

SHIZEN-HONTAI
basic natural posture

HIDARI-SHIZENTAI
left natural posture

MIGI-SHIZENTAI
right natural posture

POSTURES
Shizen-hontai is the basic natural posture: the body is relaxed, arms loosely by the sides, and the feet are no more than shoulder-width apart.

TAI-SABAKI body control
Tai-sabaki, the change of body direction by neat footwork, is the foundation of all good throwing.

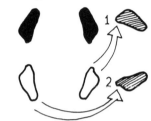

MAE-SABAKI front movement
Position one foot forward and withdraw the other so that you stand at a right-angle to the opponent's feet.

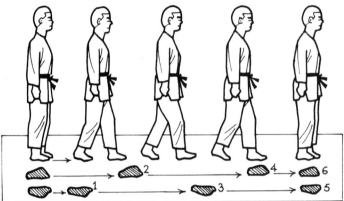

AYUMI-ASHI This is the normal pattern of walking, each foot taking alternate steps forwards (or backwards), but skimming low just above the surface of the mat rather than making high-rise steps.

USHIRO-SABAKI back movement
Retreat one foot and pivot on the other so you stand at a right-angle to your opponent's feet.

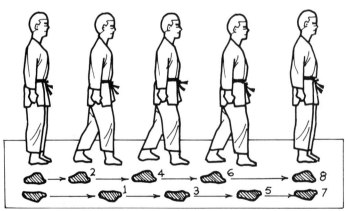

TSUGI-ASHI In this pattern of walking forwards, backwards or to either side, the skimming steps are shorter than in ayumi-ashi, with the trailing foot never quite drawing up close to the leading foot.

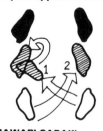

MAE-MAWARI-SABAKI
front turn-in
Advance one foot diagonally, pivot and swing the other foot around to make a 180-degree turn around so that your back is against the front of your opponent.

Rear left corner

Left side

Left front corner

Rear backward

KUZUSHI breaking balance
Applying *kuzushi*, an opponent's balance may be broken by *tori* (attacker) pulling or pushing *uke* (defender) in any direction.

Front forward

Rear right corner

Right side

Right front corner

UKEMI Breakfalls

Overcome as quickly as possible any fear of falling onto the mat from almost any angle or reasonable height. A fearless body is relaxed and is more likely to fall naturally and be less susceptible to injury than a tensed body.

Ukemi (breakfall) practice is therefore an important element of any training programme and will continue to be regularly rehearsed by all *judoka*, regardless of grade or experience, throughout their mat career. It is not only futile for good *judo*, but highly dangerous, to act as *uke* (defender) in any throwing practice, still less *randori* (free fighting practice), until the art of *ukemi* has been mastered to some degree of proficiency.

Adopt the correct attitude from the outset and you'll soon discover that good *ukemi* can be praised or even admired as much as the art of *nage-waza* (throwing techniques).

EARLY PRACTICE

Until confidence is gained, most *ukemi* may be practised at first from a kneeling posture, later from a crouch, and then finally from an upright standing posture.

SIDEWAYS ROLLING

1 From a natural standing posture, bend the left knee, drop the upper body forwards and plunge the left arm down towards the mat between the feet.

2 As the left arm and shoulder roll over the mat, the body rotates. The right arm is whipped through in a wide arc.

3 The body has completed the rotation, the head is tucked forward and the outstretched arm strikes the mat hard, palm of the hand face-down.

FORWARD ROLLING

1 Rise onto toes and drop your body forwards, with arms out, fists clenched and knees bent to spring.

2 Spring forwards onto clenched knuckles, head tucked safely sideways as you roll onto shoulders.

3 Whip arms over to break fall as soles of feet swing down to support back from impact with mat.

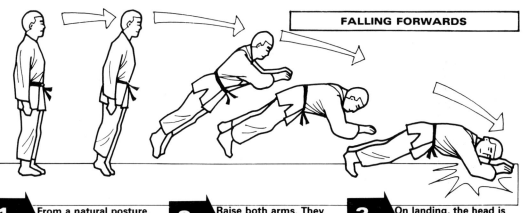

FALLING FORWARDS

1 From a natural posture, lean forwards to break your own point of balance and, with feet together and body straight, spring forwards into the air.

2 Raise both arms. They should be bent, with the elbows pointing outwards and slightly forwards; both hands should be facing palm-down.

3 On landing, the head is turned sideways for safety, legs are spreadeagled and toes are turned under to raise the knees and body clear of injury on impact.

SIDEWAYS FALLING

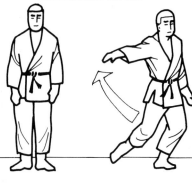

1 From a normal standing posture, swing the right arm and right leg backwards and upwards, turning the body slightly to the left.

2 Spring off the left leg into the air, looking down towards the mat as the right arm and leg swing strongly to provide momentum.

3 The head is well tucked in as the outstretched arm is swung to break the fall with the palm of the hand facing down onto the mat.

FALLING BACKWARDS

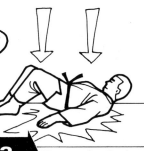

1 From a normal standing posture, raise both arms forwards and parallel to each other, and prepare to drop into a crouch.

2 From the crouch, go up onto your toes, tuck in your chin close to your chest, spring and then drop quickly backwards.

3 Hips remain raised as the initial impact is absorbed by the arms and soles of both feet, while the head is forward and safe from whiplash.

GETTING TO GRIPS

SHIZEN-TAI-NO-MIGI

opponent's left lapel and
right sleeve

JUDO-NO-KUMI-KATA

Methods of holding in *judo*

Illustrated here are most of the legitimate methods of taking a grip on an opponent during *judo*. The need to change grips occurs most commonly in either *randori* or *shiai*, and will depend upon the particular type of control your opponent necessitates or the type of technique you wish to perform. Take care, however, not to 'telegraph' your intentions with an obvious change of grip.

When actually gripping, make all your fingers work. Do not overlook (as most do!) the power of the little fingers which, if used properly, may be curled in hard and tight.

KATA-USHIRO-ERI

opponent's left sleeve an
rear right collar

RYO-OUWA-ERI

both lapels over
opponent's arms

RYO-UWA-ERI

both lapels: one arm over,
one under

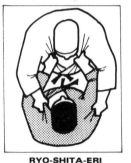

RYO-SHITA-ERI

both lapels under
opponent's arms

RYO-OUWA-WAKI

grip beneath armpits, bot
arms over

KATANAKA-WAKI

beneath armpits: one arm
over, one under

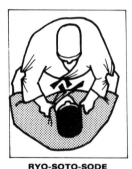

RYO-SOTO-SODE

gripping both sleeves

KATA-ERI-KATA-WAKI

one sleeve and opposite
armpit

KATA-ERI-DORI

grip one sleeve and lap
on the same side

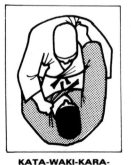

**KATA-WAKI-KARA-
USHIRO-ERI**

rear opponent's collar and
opposite armpit

RYO-OUKU-SODE

both arms out to grip
shoulders

**Grabbing the
opponent's belt in
defence is not
permitted.**

**Wrist-grabbing is
allowed only in attack
and not in defence.**

was Kenshiro Abbe (8th Dan), founder of the British Judo Council, who propounded that all motion in the Universe travels basically through a series of circular and semi-circular actions and that is only by obeying this fundamental principle of motion, avoiding stiff, angular stances or postures, that we can achieve the best *judo*.'

This principle may perhaps be applied more to *nage-waza* (throwing techniques) than to any other facet of *judo*. Standing opponents pass together through circular actions from the first movement of *kuzushi* (breaking balance), through *tsukuri* (moving the body into position for a throw) and finally into *kake* (the execution of the throw).

Throughout, the basic principle is to pull or push an opponent, if possible along an established line of energy, and thus achieve maximum effect from minimum effort. If one opponent pushes, the force is multiplied by the other pulling him further forwards and off balance, and vice versa.

The skill of *nage-waza* is in knowing not only how to throw, but *when* to throw and in *what* direction. There is a need to sense, or forecast, the direction in which an opponent is moving so that his energy may be utilised to propel him further along an existing line of force.

In that way, the act of throwing becomes both a more effective and at the same time less energy-sapping performance. The trick is in being able to forecast the direction in which an opponent is about to move his line of energy or force, or to distribute bodyweight to a point at which he may become off balance and vulnerable to a particular type of attacking throw.

Experienced players adopt different methods of forecasting an opponent's intentions. Some make the detection by watching an opponent's eyes (not always practical!), while others keep their own eyes down to watch an opponent's foot movements for changes of body direction. One of the most effective methods is to detect anticipated movements by the 'feel' or 'pull' of an opponent's jacket.

The whole range of *nage-waza* is composed of two separate categories: **tachi-waza** (standing techniques) and **sutemi-waza** (sacrifice techniques).

Tachi-waza is itself further divided into three sub-categories. They are *te-waza* (hand techniques), *ashi-waza* (foot and leg techniques) and *koshi-waza* (hip techniques).

Sutemi-waza (sacrifice techniques) are so called, because although the throwing actions start from a standing posture, they necessitate *tori* falling to the mat with *uke* in the course of executing the technique, thus 'sacrificing' himself to the prospect of groundwork.

Sutemi-waza is divided into two sub-categories. They are **ma-sutemi-waza** and **yoko-sutemi-waza**.

Ma-sutemi-waza are 'rear sacrifice techniques' which require the deliverer to fall to his rear in order to execute them. *Yoko-sutemi-waza* are 'side sacrifice techniques', because they require the deliverer to fall to either left or right side in order to execute them.

In both cases, *tori* is self-sacrificed to the prospect of groundwork (failing an 'ippon' score, which would be *sorre-made* for end of contest). It is therefore not advisable to attempt *sutemi-waza* against stronger or heavier opponents or any who have the reputation for superior groundwork. Of course, if any player is of heavy or 'rotund' build or perhaps is a mature student and less supple than a younger one, a sacrifice throw is an alternative to the more agile demands of most major *tachi-waza*. It is also a legitimate way of taking an opponent down to where physical advantages may be best exploited.

Nage-waza techniques displayed in the following *judographs* include all the techniques you need to know how to perform within the syllabus of any major judo organisation, though different associations may insert them at different stages of examination progress through the *kyu* grades to Black Belt (1st Dan) standard.

The main centre line of each *judograph* sets out the stages of each technique in numerical sequence. At an appropriate stage, the critical path breaks away above this to show counter or combination techniques as (a), (b), (c), etc. These are not deep or difficult counter techniques. They are basic and sometimes repetitive, simply because they suit several occasions. Their main purpose is to serve as a reminder that, in the event of *uke* effectively blocking an attack, *tori* can still keep his initial energy investment in work by carrying it on into an alternative but continued attacking technique.

Certainly, the basic techniques must be mastered separately, but in practice try to avoid using them in isolation, one from the other. Try from the outset to sustain attack by, if necessary, moving from one into another. Apart from remembering (for *most* effective results) to keep moving in the direction of established lines of energy force, there is no hard and fast rule about which technique combines with another.

On the one hand, there are those who specialise in combination techniques and are able to demonstrate the principle by lengthy sequences of one move into another. They would admit, though, that if your opponent is still upright after, say, a second stage of attack, maybe there's something wrong with your *judo* and you should turn out and start again anyway.

Once you've grasped the principle, you will with a bit of practice and experience develop your own special combination techniques which will help you acquire a good standard of *judo* performance.

O-GOSHI Major hip throw

Comprising, as it does, so many basic elements of skill, *o-goshi* is an excellent throw for the beginner to master before going on to other *koshi-waza* (hip techniques).

It is necessary for *tori* to develop neat footwork in order to move through a full 180 degrees so that he finishes up with his feet close together, between those of *uke* and facing in the same direction as *uke*. *Tori*'s body establishes firm contact as his hips are driven backwards, squarely into *uke*'s body. *Tori*'s knees bend in readiness for lift-off and the arm encircling his opponent pulls *uke* further onto him.

One problem in applying *o-goshi* during *randori* or *shiai* is being able to free the encircling arm from *uke*'s sleeve grip in order to slip it through his armpit and across his back. A solution is to release your grip on his lapel, passing that hand down and then upwards and over the outside of the elbow of *uke*'s restricting arm in order to grip his jacket at the armpit. His elbow will become locked and he should release his grip and enable you to slip your arm around his back.

a This is where *uke* attempts to foil *tori*'s attack by dropping his centre of gravity and stepping around the outside of *tori*'s legs, but...

1 *Tori* and *uke* are facing as *tori* pulls *uke* forwards and moves his right foot diagonally across to a point just inside the line of *uke*'s right foot.

2 *Tori* slips his right hand through *uke*'s left armpit, simultaneously pivoting on his right foot and pulling hard on *uke*'s right sleeve.

3 *Tori* completes the pivot, with maximum body contact as both hips drive squarely into *uke* who is drawn further forward by *tori*'s strong arm actions.

Some players choose to assist their *o-goshi* at this stage of the throw by grabbing the back of their opponent's belt as in *tsuri-goshi* (*see* pages 30–1).

b ...*tori* hesitates, feints and raises his own right leg...

c ...to sweep it up the outside of *uke*'s right leg, pivoting towards his own left...

d ...and throwing his opponent with *harai-goshi* (*see* pages 28–9).

4 *Tori* continues turning, straightening his legs to help raise *uke* clear of the mat, still pushing with his right arm and pulling with the left.

5 *Tori* completes his body turn as *uke* is pulled around to roll off his hips, but *uke* is still being controlled by *tori*'s arm action.

6 *Uke* clears *tori*'s hips to breakfall at the feet of *tori* who rightly retains control of the arm in readiness to drop into groundwork.

This front view shows how *tori* pulls *uke* in close to revolve around his hips as he turns his head to look in the direction of the intended landing area on the mat. They say in *judo* that if you turn the head, the rest will follow!

HANE-GOSHI Spring hip throw

The proper execution of *hane-goshi* demands complete co-ordination of hand, hip and leg movements to achieve the 'spring' action of the throw.

As the instep of *tori*'s rising leg locks in against the inside ankle, or calf, of *uke*'s leg, the knee is bent and brought forwards so that *tori* can make full control with his outer thigh, hip and chest in line against *uke*'s body as it is drawn forwards. Simultaneously *tori* leans forwards, pushing upwards and backwards until his bent knee straightens and, as he turns his upper body in the direction of the intended throw, *uke* is 'sprung' off his twisting hip.

Once perfected, *hane-goshi* is a good contest technique, especially if combined with *makikomi* (*see* pages 96–7).

One story attributes much of the early popularity of this throw to Yoshiaki Yamashita, one of the early disciples to teach *Kodokan judo* outside Japan in the early 1900s and who had the US President Theodore Roosevelt among his students.

a At this point, *uke* may attempt resistance by, for instance, planting his feet firmly on the mat and pulling backwards...

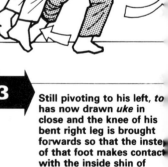

1 *Tori* withdraws his left hip and leg to maximise the pull as his left arm draws *uke* off balance to his right front corner, forcing *uke* to put his right foot forward in an attempt to correct his balance.

2 *Tori* transfers his right hand grip to the back of *uke*'s collar as he continues to draw *uke* further off balance over his supporting right leg, pivoting on his own left foot as he begins turning in on his opponent.

3 Still pivoting to his left, *to* has now drawn *uke* in close and the knee of his bent right leg is brought forwards so that the instep of that foot makes contact with the inside shin of *uke*'s right leg.

b ...which provokes *tori* to feint and to attack again immediately, but with a high, circular right arm action...

c ...which increases the power of his body's revolving momentum...

d ...and enables him to throw *uke* with a powerful *hane-makikomi* (*see* pages 96–7).

4 As *tori* leans forwards, his right leg sweeps back, upwards and straightening so that *uke* is raised clear of the mat.

5 At the maximum point of his leg swing, *tori*'s leg is almost straight and he twists his hips to 'spring' *uke* clear of his body.

6 Aided by his strong arm action, *tori* carries *uke* around and retains arm control as *uke* breakfalls in front of him.

As an alternative to taking a grip behind the collar for this technique, some players feel they can generate more lifting power in the throw by slipping the arm through *uke*'s armpit and grasping the jacket high up behind the shoulder.

TSURI-KOMI-GOSHI Resisting hip throw

Generally referred to in English as the 'resisting hip throw', the alternative 'lift-pull hip throw' is probably more explicit of the action involved. The initial application is similar to *o-goshi* in so much as *tori* uses *uke*'s own advancing momentum to draw him further forwards and off-balance. As he does so, *tori* makes a full 180-degree turn in order to place his hips against *uke* so that he finishes facing in the same direction as his opponent prior to going fully into the technique.

Instead of encircling *uke*'s body with his drawing arm, as in *o-goshi*, *tori* retains hold of *uke*'s lapel, drawing it upwards and forwards as he crouches low to pull through and complete the throw.

The lower *tori* is able to crouch as he turns in, the more effective will be the eventual throw as *uke* is drawn forwards over a low point of balance. It is the low-pivot action of *tsuri-komi-goshi* that makes it such a useful technique against a taller or heavier opponent. Such opponents are often vulnerable to what might loosely be referred to as these 'low-level' attacks.

a Instead of grasping *uke*'s left lapel, *tori* may choose to grasp the underside of *uke*'s left sleeve with his right hand...

1 *Tori* pulls *uke* forwards, placing his right foot across diagonally to a spot just on the inside line of *uke*'s advancing right foot, and withdrawing his left hip and leg in preparation for a full pivot to his left.

2 As *tori* completes the pivoting turn-in, his left arm pulls strongly on *uke*'s right sleeve and his right hand has taken a firm, strong grip of *uke*'s left lapel in readiness to assist the left.

3 *Tori* has completed the turn-in, legs crouching as he pulls to the left with left arm and begins to pull upwards and forwards with his right.

◁ ...pulling this arm overhead as he turns...

C ▷ ...to throw *uke* with a variation of *tsuri-komi-goshi*, which is called *sode-tsuri-komi-goshi*.

◀ *Tori* has driven his hips into the opponent, straightened his legs, pulled with his left hand and driven upwards with his right as *uke* clears the mat.

5 ▷ Driving through strongly with his extending right arm, *tori* turns *uke* around him with his left and the throw is executed.

6 ▷ *Uke* is pulled round to land at *tori*'s feet, with *tori* still well-balanced, in control and ready for groundwork if necessary.

From a different angle, this shows how *tori*'s right arm is extending and pulling *uke* forwards and up onto his back.

UKI-GOSHI Floating hip throw

This simple and yet so effective technique was devised by Professor Jigoro Kano himself and therefore provides a typical example of how maximum results may be achieved from minimum concentrated effort, providing *tori*'s timing is correct.

At first glance, beginners may perhaps be forgiven for mistaking *uki-goshi* for *o-goshi*, but there are in fact wide differences between the two techniques.

When executing the more subtle *uki-goshi*, *tori* does not turn so far in that *both* of his hips are against *uke*'s abdomen, his knees are no more bent than when standing in normal posture and neither does he raise his hips to assist the throw.

Maybe the only two similarities between the techniques are that *tori* turns in to face (almost!) in the same direction as *uke* and that he also slips an arm beneath *uke*'s armpit and around his back.

However, in *uki-goshi*, *tori* pivots on his lead foot to swing his other foot onto the outside of *uke*'s feet, with only his lead hip being driven in against *uke*'s outer hip.

a At this stage, *uke* might willingly move in the direction of *tori*'s pulling movement, using its momentum to help him step around the line of *tori*'s feet and maybe int countering technique...

1 As *tori* draws *uke* forwards, he prepares to bring his own right foot across diagonally to a spot on the mat roughly between *uke*'s two feet.

2 *Tori* drives his right hip to the inside of *uke*'s left hip, slipping his right arm through *uke*'s armpit, pivoting on the right foot, and pulling on *uke*'s right sleeve.

3 *Tori*'s right hand reache round towards *uke*'s far hip, completing the pivo with his left foot swung the far outside of *uke*'s feet.

Tori may drive the upper part of his encircling arm up into *uke*'s armpit to increase the power of what is a subtle lift-and-pull arm action. This is particularly helpful against opponents shorter than yourself.

▶ ...but before he can apply any counter of his own, *tori* uses that same momentum to help him continue pivoting to his left...

c ▶ ...sweeping his right leg up the inside of *uke*'s left thigh...

d ▶ ...and throwing *uke* with *uchi-mata* (*see* pages 66–7).

▶ Pulled in close to *tori*'s right hip, *uke* is now well unbalanced and *tori* is able to continue pulling with his left arm and pushing with his right, so that *uke* is twirled around the hip...

5 ▶ ...*tori* giving the hip a final quick twist to throw *uke* clear of his body...

6 ▶ ...and floating through the air to breakfall on the mat in front of *tori*.

HARAI-GOSHI Sweeping loin throw

Once perfected, *harai-goshi* can be a powerful contest technique, especially for the lean, long-legged competitor possessing natural physical attributes.

History relates that one early *judoka*, Shiro Sago, was reputedly able to devise a counter attack against any technique. However, Professor Jigoro Kano apparently used his famous *uki-goshi* technique against him with considerable success for some time before Sago developed a way of almost jumping around Kano and countering with what eventually became harai-goshi.

Harai-goshi remains a useful counter attack to any opponent who steps in close to execute some other technique, as later pages of this book will demonstrate.

Whether used as a counter or as a major attacking technique in its own right, *harai-goshi* should be a strong, well-balanced movement devoid of any chopping action with the sweeping leg. Retention of *tori*'s body balance will be helped by him pivoting well round on the supporting foot and swivelling his upper body and head in the direction of the throw.

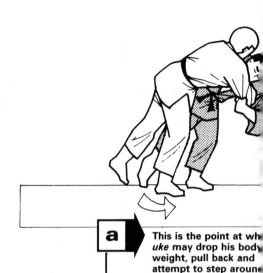

a This is the point at wh uke may drop his body weight, pull back and attempt to step aroun tori's leg before it can threaded through to st its sweeping action, so

1 *Tori* steps back, withdrawing his left hip and leg to strengthen the pull on *uke*'s right arm. This breaks *uke*'s balance to the right front corner and forces him to attempt the correction of his balance by stepping forwards with his right foot.

2 As *uke* is pulled further forwards, *tori* pivots on his left foot. He continues to pull through with his left hand on *uke*'s sleeve and (if preferred) moves his right hand from *uke*'s lapel to take a grip behind the jacket collar.

3 Body contact is establi and, as *tori* continues pulling *uke* forwards, h right leg has been draw through to begin a swe up the outside of *uke*'s right leg.

The sweeping leg should initially cross the leg of an opponent at a point slightly above the knee, or just below the knee if competing against a much taller opponent. Either way, avoid striking the knee itself, as this can easily cause serious injury.

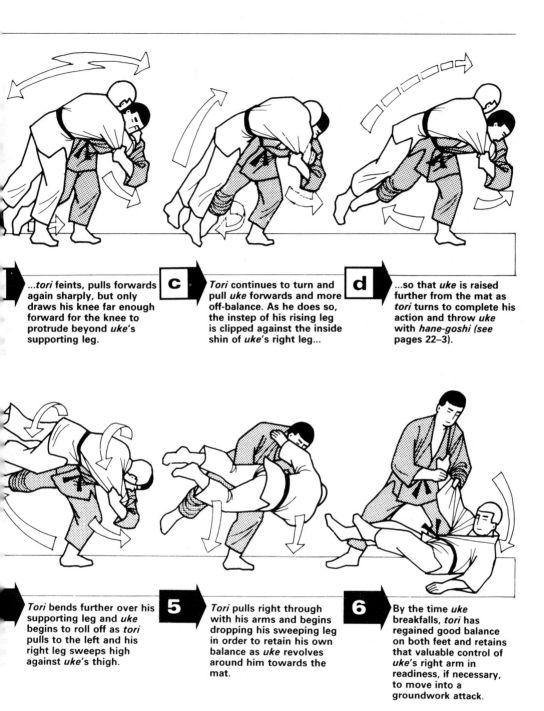

▶ ...*tori* feints, pulls forwards again sharply, but only draws his knee far enough forward for the knee to protrude beyond *uke*'s supporting leg.

c ▶ *Tori* continues to turn and pull *uke* forwards and more off-balance. As he does so, the instep of his rising leg is clipped against the inside shin of *uke*'s right leg...

d ▶ ...so that *uke* is raised further from the mat as *tori* turns to complete his action and throw *uke* with *hane-goshi* (*see pages 22–3*).

▶ *Tori* bends further over his supporting leg and *uke* begins to roll off as *tori* pulls to the left and his right leg sweeps high against *uke*'s thigh.

5 ▶ *Tori* pulls right through with his arms and begins dropping his sweeping leg in order to retain his own balance as *uke* revolves around him towards the mat.

6 ▶ By the time *uke* breakfalls, *tori* has regained good balance on both feet and retains that valuable control of *uke*'s right arm in readiness, if necessary, to move into a groundwork attack.

TSURI-GOSHI Lifting hip throw

Tsuri-goshi is really a variation of the basic *o-goshi*, but with *tori* making a deliberate attempt from the outset to assist the throw by grabbing and pulling upwards and forwards on the back of an opponent's belt.

There are two forms of *tsuri-goshi*. Shown here is the form known as *kotsuri-goshi* (small hip throw) in which *tori*'s drawing arm is slipped beneath *uke*'s armpit and around his back in order to grab the belt to give extra power in pulling *uke* forwards and off balance. This is useful against opponents of similar or taller stature than your own.

The other form of *tsuri-goshi* is called *utsuri-goshi* (large hip throw), and to perform this *tori* passes his lead arm over *uke*'s shoulder to reach downwards for the back of the belt. This form is useful against a smaller opponent, or one who adopts a low crouching, defensive posture.

a It's not uncommon, at t[his] stage, for *uke* to attemp[t] foiling *tori*'s attack by using the momentum o[f] the turn-in to pull hims[elf] around *tori*'s legs...

1 *Tori* withdraws his left hip and leg to help draw *uke* forwards. His right foot is already in position and is ready for a pivot to his own left.

2 As he pivots to turn in, *tori*'s hand slips through *uke*'s left armpit to grasp the back of *uke*'s belt in order to assist in drawing him in close.

3 *Tori*'s hips drive into u[ke] the turn is complete, w[ith] the knees slightly ben[t] the right hand graspin[g] back of *uke*'s belt.

Because *uke* is crouching low, he presents *tori* with a golden opportunity to reach over his shoulder to grasp the back of the belt in the *otsuri-goshi* (large hip throw) form of *tsuri-goshi*.

From this over-arm grip on the belt, *tori* is able to exert powerful pulling power as he turns to raise *uke* onto his hips, completing the rest of the throw as for the *kotsuri-goshi* form shown above.

b ...in which case *tori* may retain his *tsuri-goshi* hand grips, but might begin to draw up his knee...

c ...he may clip his instep close against the inside of *uke*'s shin...

d ...while continuing to pull *uke* forwards and around as he raises the instep of his bent leg against *uke*'s inside shin so that, using the leg action of *hane-goshi* (*see* pages 22–3), he is able to throw *uke* to the mat.

Tori pulls *uke* onto his hips, straightening his knees to assist lift and continuing to pull with the left as he turns to the left.

5 *Uke* is finally rolled around *tori*'s hips, aided by *tori*'s upper body twist and strong arm actions controlling his flight towards the mat.

6 *Tori* releases the grip on *uke*'s belt mid-flight and both his hands are brought to control *uke*'s right arm as he breakfalls in front of *tori*.

USHIRO-GOSHI Rear hip throw

c *Tori*'s balance is broken to his rear right corner as *uke* pushes through and he breakfalls as *uke* follows up with attacking groundwork.

b *Uke* then sweeps that leg forwards to clip the back of *tori*'s right heel, sweeping it away as he pushes off his left foot.

a If *tori* hesitates, *uke* may easily be the one to continue on to a combination technique by swinging his left leg backwards between *tori*'s legs.

1 *Tori* and *uke* are facing each other as *uke* attempts to break *tori*'s balance to his right front corner, pulling on *tori*'s right sleeve and forcing him to re-balance by advancing his right foot forwards.

2 *Tori* is already sensing his opponent's intention to perform a hip technique (say, *tsuri-goshi*), so he steps his left leg to a spot behind and roughly between *uke*'s legs. He now faces forward in almost the same direction as his attacker.
Tori simultaneously crouches to lower his bodyweight, allowing his abdomen to become wedged in below *uke*'s hip-line as he reaches his right arm across the front of *uke*'s body.

3 Gripping *uke*'s jacket at front and his belt at the back, *tori* pushes his abdomen and hips forwards and upwards, hard against *uke*'s body begin raising him clear the mat.

iro-goshi is a dramatic yet ideal technique n which to block or counter an attack which olves an opponent having to turn in on you in er to execute his own technique. It is particu-/ useful against any hip technique attack, ugh it is critical to counter at the right split ond or you may become the victim of a nter attack yourself (as demonstrated in strations (a), (b) and (c) opposite).

ssential requirements for the execution of *iro-goshi* are: (i) the alertness to react at the cal moment the technique may be best cuted; (ii) good timing in this respect; and (iii) speed and strength to carry it out. As already

explained, failure to react at the critical moment might easily make you vulnerable to a counter attack yourself. Note, though, that this particular advice can be applied to any action you may care to take in *judo*.

On top of that, strength is required to ensure that the technique is performed at speed, leaving your opponent with no time to wriggle or turn out of the lift.

All these aspects of performance must be combined and co-ordinated into one smooth movement. Obviously, it's not a technique to attempt in competition against an opponent much heavier than yourself.

Tori straightens his legs and his back arches as the lift is completed. *Uke* is thrust clear off *tori*'s hip.

5 **Tori** controls *uke*'s flight to the mat, withdrawing his left leg slightly to avoid any collision with *uke*'s fall.

6 **Tori** retains full control as *uke* breakfalls in front of him.

This reverse view shows how *tori* thrusts *uke* up clear of his left hip, assisting the lift by his strong grip on the back of *uke*'s belt.

UTSURI-GOSHI Changing hip throw

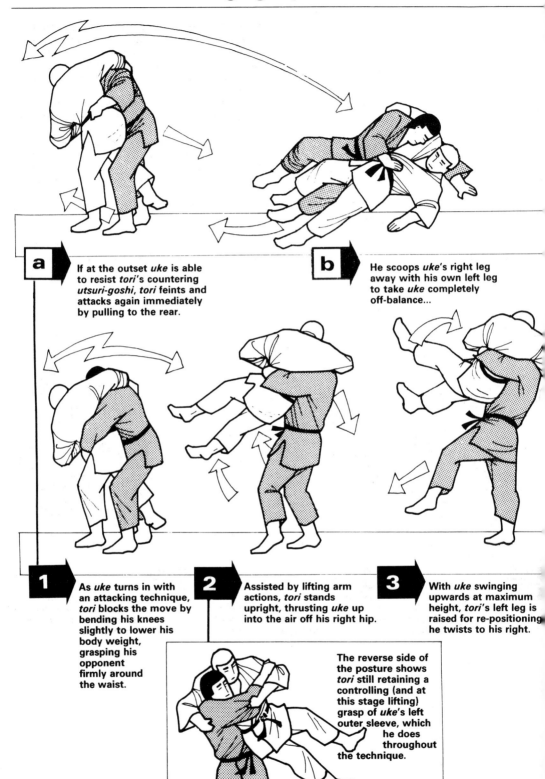

a If at the outset *uke* is able to resist *tori*'s countering *utsuri-goshi*, *tori* feints and attacks again immediately by pulling to the rear.

b He scoops *uke*'s right leg away with his own left leg to take *uke* completely off-balance...

1 As *uke* turns in with an attacking technique, *tori* blocks the move by bending his knees slightly to lower his body weight, grasping his opponent firmly around the waist.

2 Assisted by lifting arm actions, *tori* stands upright, thrusting *uke* up into the air off his right hip.

3 With *uke* swinging upwards at maximum height, *tori*'s left leg is raised for re-positioning he twists to his right.

The reverse side of the posture shows *tori* still retaining a controlling (and at this stage lifting) grasp of *uke*'s left outer sleeve, which he does throughout the technique.

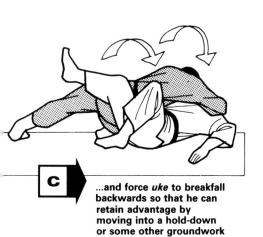

Utsuri-goshi is another spectacular counter-attacking technique which is mainly successful against hip technique attacks. Once again, it requires a snap choice of the critical moment, good timing, speed and strength in order to make it effective.

Utsuri-goshi is not recommended for use against taller opponents or those much heavier than yourself. However, it is not uncommon to see *utsuri-goshi* attempted by those who have not devoted to it the practice required to achieve anywhere near effective perfection, or who even possess the natural physical attributes required to make that possible. Although there are doubtless those who may wish to contradict, *utsuri-goshi* (and to a lesser extent *ushiro-goshi*) is the technique of the confident, strong player.

Confidence, though, comes not entirely from strength, but from the knowledge that in support of it there has been much practice to perfect all the other ingredients of the throw.

C ...and force *uke* to breakfall backwards so that he can retain advantage by moving into a hold-down or some other groundwork technique.

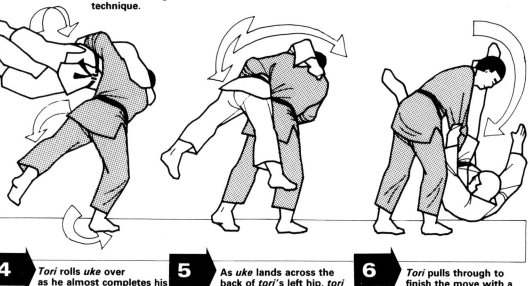

4 *Tori* rolls *uke* over as he almost completes his turn to the right, his left foot now coming down to restore his balance.

5 As *uke* lands across the back of *tori*'s left hip, *tori* continues pulling hard round to his right with strong arm actions.

6 *Tori* pulls through to finish the move with a basic hip throw and *uke* breakfalls to the mat in front of him.

KOSHI-GURUMA Hip-wheel throw

When turning in to perform *koshi-guruma*, *tori* may employ much the same foot movements as for *o-goshi*. His body makes a similar 180-degree turnabout to face in the same direction as his opponent, but the right hip is driven much further across to protrude almost beyond *uke*'s right hip.

Some players favour the encircling arm being slipped beneath *uke*'s armpit, as for *o-goshi*, but if that is the case then it must be clamped high against *uke*'s opposite back shoulder and not lower down on the hip or belt.

The more usual and effective use of the encircling arm for *koshi-guruma* is to take it over *uke*'s shoulder to grip either the back of the jacket collar or to go right across and grip the far opposite shoulder of the jacket. Either grip provides a high point of pull as *tori* bends to draw *uke* close into the back of his hips.

Too many beginners make the mistake of almost recklessly slamming their encircling arm around the back of *uke*'s neck to clamp their opponent in what is virtually an illegal neck lock. Still worse, to throw an opponent whilst in such a neck lock is highly dangerous and contrary to the spirit of *judo*.

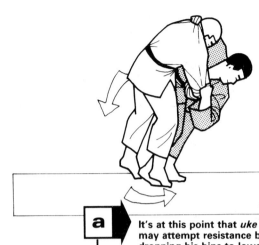

a It's at this point that *uke* may attempt resistance by dropping his hips to lower his centre of gravity and stepping his right leg forwards.

1 *Tori* breaks *uke*'s balance to the front as he starts to bring his right foot forwards and across in the direction of *uke*'s right foot.

2 *Tori* positions his right foot at a point inside the line of *uke*'s right foot and prepares to pivot as his right arm circles behind *uke*'s shoulders.

3 The pivot completed, *tori*'s hips are driven firmly into *uke* who is drawn forward as *tori* bends to pull him in close, assisted by strong arm action.

This is the point at which *tori*'s encircling arm must, if he's not going for a back-of-the-collar grip, be pushed to the far shoulder and not, as shown here, become wrapped around *uke*'s neck. A neck lock is dangerous, illegal and not permitted in *judo*.

b ➤ Particularly if *tori* has already opted for a back-of-the-collar grip, he's ideally positioned to change tactics by sweeping with his right leg...

c ➤ ...which drives up the inside of *uke*'s left thigh...

d ➤ ...to complete *uchi-mata* (*see* pages 66–7).

4 ➤ *Tori* straightens to carry *uke* clear of the mat as he turns his own upper body left.

5 ➤ *Tori* continues turning his upper body to the left in the direction of the throw.

6 ➤ *Uke* has circled around *tori*'s hips to breakfall in front of *tori* who retains hold of that right arm in readiness to proceed into groundwork.

This front view shows how tightly *tori* has pulled his opponent across both hips so that *uke* revolves in a circular and controlled motion around his body.

SUKUI-NAGE Scooping throw

Sukui-nage is a good technique to apply at the critical moment when you have successfully foiled an opponent's attack and he is in the process of turning out from you.

Even then, it is a technique recommended for use only by those possessing the confidence and strength required to make it effective. Once embarked upon, *tori* must be full of positive commitment, working at speed to complete the technique before *uke* realises just what's happening.

Repeatedly practise *sukui-nage* to: develop a smooth step-around your opponent; work on raising his sleeve as you pull it round at a high enough level to slip your arm clearly across his body; establish strong hip contact; discover whether you find grasping the outside of his trousers more effective than the bottom of his jacket to provide a point of lift; work out whether you prefer to slip your arm under or over his arm to reach across his body; see whether you release his arm altogether and take a good grip on each side of his trouser hip to make the best lift...

The important thing is to rehearse all variations, remembering that *sukui-nage* is a surprise attack technique you'll be launching at the most opportune moment.

a Because *tori* senses immediately that *uke* is about to drop his bodyweight in resistance the *sukui-nage* attack, to begins a swing of his left leg...

1 *Tori* has successfully blocked an attack and *uke* still has momentum to his right as he circles out, but remains held close in by *tori*'s sleeve grip.

2 *Tori* pivots on his right foot to place his left behind *uke*, pulling on *uke*'s left sleeve and passing his right arm across *uke*'s body.

3 *Tori* crouches to drive his hip firmly in against *uke* pulling *uke* solidly into h and taking a strong grip trouser at *uke*'s far hip.

If *tori* prefers, the arm crossing *uke*'s body may pass over the top of *uke*'s arm in order to grip the far side of his *judogi*.

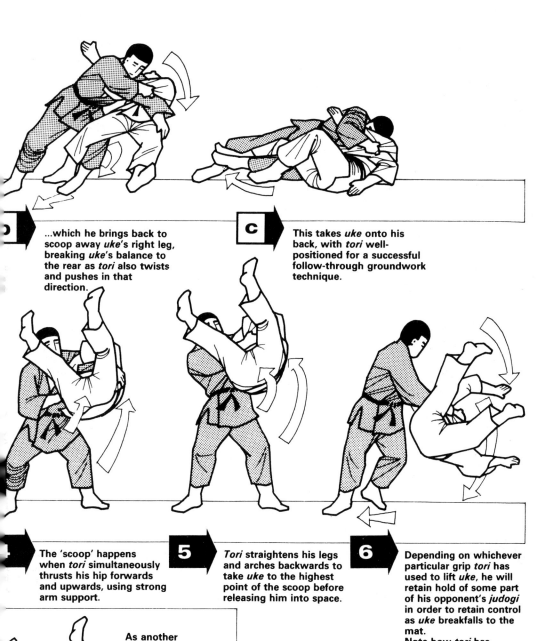

...which he brings back to scoop away *uke*'s right leg, breaking *uke*'s balance to the rear as *tori* also twists and pushes in that direction.

c This takes *uke* onto his back, with *tori* well-positioned for a successful follow-through groundwork technique.

The 'scoop' happens when *tori* simultaneously thrusts his hip forwards and upwards, using strong arm support.

5 *Tori* straightens his legs and arches backwards to take *uke* to the highest point of the scoop before releasing him into space.

6 Depending on whichever particular grip *tori* has used to lift *uke*, he will retain hold of some part of his opponent's *judogi* in order to retain control as *uke* breakfalls to the mat.

Note how *tori* has slightly withdrawn his left leg in order to avoid collision and possible injury to either player as *uke* heads for the mat.

As another alternative, *tori* may choose to release *uke*'s sleeve and go for the more direct lift-power derived from a grip on either side of *uke*'s outer hips or outer upper thighs.

TAI-O-TOSHI Body drop

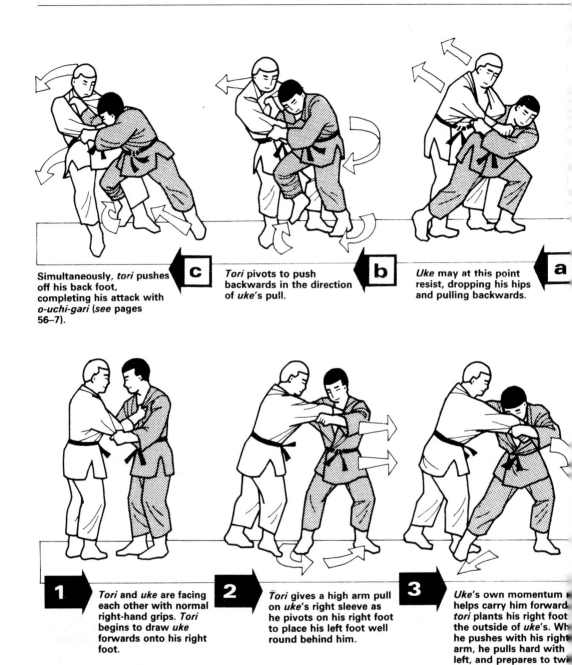

c Simultaneously, *tori* pushes off his back foot, completing his attack with *o-uchi-gari* (*see* pages 56–7).

b *Tori* pivots to push backwards in the direction of *uke*'s pull.

a *Uke* may at this point resist, dropping his hips and pulling backwards.

1 *Tori* and *uke* are facing each other with normal right-hand grips. *Tori* begins to draw *uke* forwards onto his right foot.

2 *Tori* gives a high arm pull on *uke*'s right sleeve as he pivots on his right foot to place his left foot well round behind him.

3 *Uke*'s own momentum helps carry him forward. *tori* plants his right foot the outside of *uke*'s. Wh he pushes with his right arm, he pulls hard with left, and prepares to tw his body to his right.

though categorised as *te-waza* (hand technique), many parts of a *judoka*'s anatomy need to synchronised and working in harmony in order execute *tai-o-toshi*. Hands, hips, legs and head come into play, although there is no actual ain body contact during the performance of the ow.

Tai-o-toshi is a classic *judo* technique requiring, en once perfected, only a minimum of energy vestment for maximum return. It is ideal for use ainst taller or heavier opposition, depending as does for success upon the exploitation of an ponent's own forward momentum and the low ntre of gravity over which he is pulled into the ow.

Whether in *randori* or *shiai*, many opportunities occur to use this technique repeatedly as a direct attack, as a counter or to work in with a sequence of combination techniques.

Economy of energy involved makes *tai-o-toshi* a well-used and popular contest technique. However, laziness is one reason why too many players (especially beginners) don't make the technique work as well as it might, or even at all. This is reflected in failure to bend low enough over the supporting front leg or to continue turning the body fully around in the direction of the throw, thereby maximising power to the hands and arms as they pull through to tip an opponent over the outstretched leg.

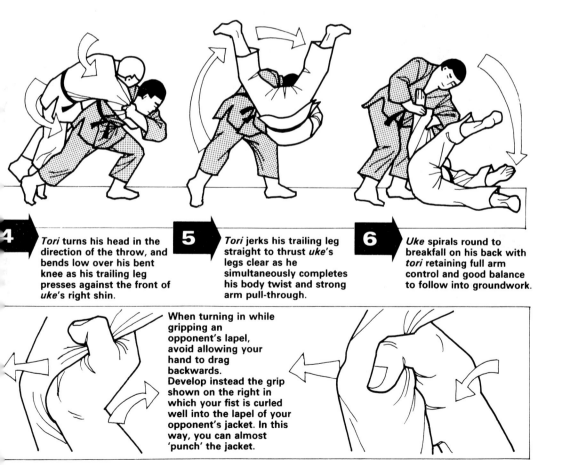

4 *Tori* turns his head in the direction of the throw, and bends low over his bent knee as his trailing leg presses against the front of *uke*'s right shin.

5 *Tori* jerks his trailing leg straight to thrust *uke*'s legs clear as he simultaneously completes his body twist and strong arm pull-through.

6 *Uke* spirals round to breakfall on his back with *tori* retaining full arm control and good balance to follow into groundwork.

When turning in while gripping an opponent's lapel, avoid allowing your hand to drag backwards. Develop instead the grip shown on the right in which your fist is curled well into the lapel of your opponent's jacket. In this way, you can almost 'punch' the jacket.

IPPON-SEOI-NAGE One-arm shoulder throw

While in the process of learning to perform *ippon-seoi-nage*, the foot movements take *tori*'s body through a 180-degree revolution in steps similar to those employed in *o-goshi* and other hip techniques. However, remember that *ippon-seoi-nage* is not a *hip* technique, but a *hand* technique, and that the need for maximum body contact is not so crucial a requirement for success.

Some body contact is required, however, if only to provide a fulcrum over which *uke* may be pulled off-balance as *tori* turns in to propel him forwards, upwards and around his own shoulder. In fact, the lower *tori* crouches on his turn-in, the lower will be the fulcrum and the more effective the ultimate technique. This is what makes *ippon-seoi-nage* so useful against taller or heavier opponents than you. Their centre of gravity is already higher than your own, making them vulnerable to a 'low-lying' attack such as this.

A correct performance of *ippon-seoi-nage* again symbolises the true art of *judo* as *tori* turns in at precisely the moment *uke* is advancing towards him. This enables *tori* to utilise *uke*'s energy force as an aid to propelling him into the throw.

a ▶ *Uke* may try to foil *tori*'s attack at this point by attempting to step around *tori*'s hip.

1 ▶ *Tori* withdraws his left hip and leg to assist his arm pull as he breaks *uke*'s balance forward, reaching to position his right foot just inside the line of *uke*'s right foot.

2 ▶ As *tori* pivots on his right foot, swinging his left foot round behind him, he turns in to slip his right arm beneath *uke*'s right arm.

3 ▶ Having pivoted through 1 degrees on bent knees, *tor* pulls hard on *uke*'s right sleeve while his own righ upper arm drives up beneath *uke*'s armpit.

To overcome resistance at this point, or to help cope with a heavy opponent, *tori* may close in with his right hand to grasp *uke*'s jacket and pull on it to add power to the technique.

Either way, *tori* should never allow *uke*'s upper arm, or armpit, to ride so high up his own upper arm that it's on top of his shoulder.

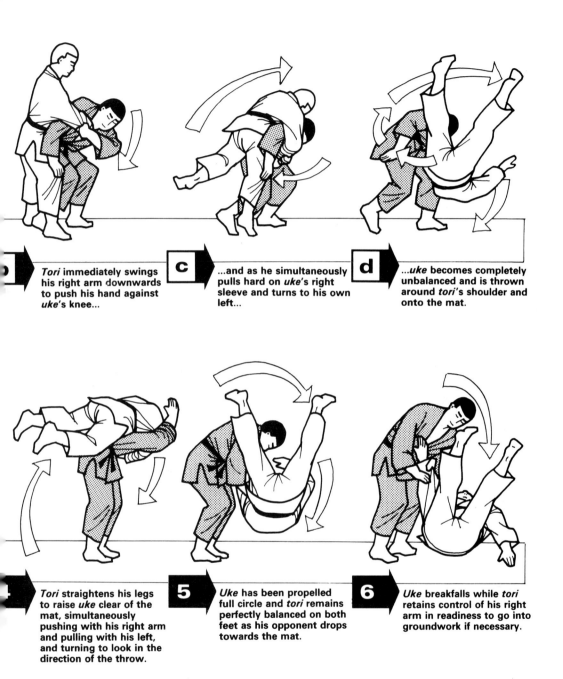

Tori immediately swings his right arm downwards to push his hand against *uke*'s knee...

c ...and as he simultaneously pulls hard on *uke*'s right sleeve and turns to his own left...

d ...*uke* becomes completely unbalanced and is thrown around *tori*'s shoulder and onto the mat.

Tori straightens his legs to raise *uke* clear of the mat, simultaneously pushing with his right arm and pulling with his left, and turning to look in the direction of the throw.

5 *Uke* has been propelled full circle and *tori* remains perfectly balanced on both feet as his opponent drops towards the mat.

6 *Uke* breakfalls while *tori* retains control of his right arm in readiness to go into groundwork if necessary.

MOROTE-SEOI-NAGE Two-arm shoulder throw

Morote-seoi-nage is the form of *seoi-nage* listed in the Kodokan *Gokyo*, which is a syllabus of standard throwing techniques. However, the great similarity it shares with the other form, *ippon-seoi-nage* (*see* pages 42–3) is that although the execution of both depends upon *tori* making a full 180-degree turn-in to face the same direction as *uke*, neither of them is a hip technique – they are both hand techniques.

Another similarity is the manner in which *tori* turns-in at the critical moment in order to utilise the oncoming energy of the advancing *uke* as an aid to propelling him into the throw. Also, because of their increased effectiveness when applied from a low point of gravity, both are useful techniques for use against tall opponents.

Of course, the obvious main difference between the two techniques is *tori*'s use of the right arm (or left arm if performing a left-handed technique). In fact, one problem sometimes encountered with *morote-seoi-nage* is being able to free the arm from *uke*'s sleeve grip in order to move it across the front of *uke* so that the elbow may be pushed upwards to fit beneath *uke*'s armpit.

a As *uke* has been able to resist *tori*'s initial attac[k] *tori* feints as though to [break?] out, but attacks again immediately, surprising [uke] by dropping to one kne[e as] he turns-in again.

1 *Tori* and *uke* are facing in normal right-hand postures, with *tori* walking to his rear as *uke* is pulled forwards.

2 *Tori* moves his right foot diagonally toward *uke*'s while simultaneously pivoting to swing his left foot around to the rear.

3 As *tori* completes a full 180-degree pivot, his ri[ght] elbow drives into *uke*'s armpit. He pulls to his l[eft] and *uke* is raised off-balance forwards.

On the right, *tori* pulls on *uke*'s sleeve and prepares to drive his right forearm, close in across the front of *uke*'s chest.

On the right, *tori* has used the power of his turning shoulder to help break *uke*'s left-hand grip as he curls in his wrist to grip *uke*'s lapel and drive his elbow across and up into *uke*'s armpit.

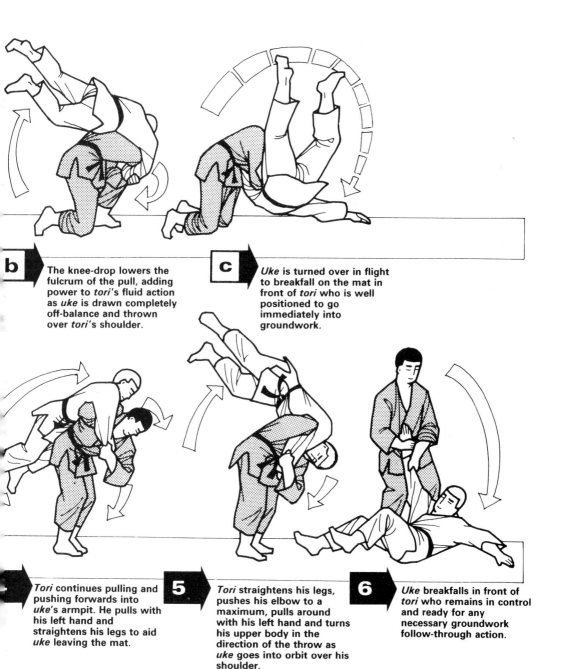

b The knee-drop lowers the fulcrum of the pull, adding power to *tori*'s fluid action as *uke* is drawn completely off-balance and thrown over *tori*'s shoulder.

c *Uke* is turned over in flight to breakfall on the mat in front of *tori* who is well positioned to go immediately into groundwork.

Tori continues pulling and pushing forwards into *uke*'s armpit. He pulls with his left hand and straightens his legs to aid *uke* leaving the mat.

5 *Tori* straightens his legs, pushes his elbow to a maximum, pulls around with his left hand and turns his upper body in the direction of the throw as *uke* goes into orbit over his shoulder.

6 *Uke* breakfalls in front of *tori* who remains in control and ready for any necessary groundwork follow-through action.

MOROTE-SEOI-TOSHI Shoulder drop

The most distinctive and obvious identification of a *morote-seoi-toshi* technique is that it combines the arm movements of *morote-seoi-nage* (*see* pages 44–5) with the leg movements of *tai-otoshi* (*see* pages 40–1).

It is, of course, a hand-throw technique, depending as it does for effectiveness upon *tori* turning in to attack at the critical moment he is able to exploit the oncoming force of his opponent's own energy.

As shown, *tori* may overcome *uke*'s first resistance to the initial *morote-seoi-toshi* attack by whipping into an *o-soto-gari* or making some other combination move. Alternatively, *tori* could feint, re-attack and drop to one knee to deliver his throw in much the same way as shown for *morote-seoi-nage* (*see* pages 44–5). If you ever choose to drop to the knee, then it must be a fluid part of a non-stop rolling movement and not part of a stop-go dragging action. Also, a 'dead' drop onto the knee can be the cause of injury.

Morote-seoi-toshi can also be a good follow-through combination to a failed *morote-seoi-nage* attack. *Tori* would half turn-out from his failed *morote-seoi-nage* and then surprise his opponent by whipping back in with a low-level *morote-seoi-toshi* technique.

a This is the point at whi
uke may pull back to re
tori's attack, attemptin
transfer his weight ont
left foot...

1 Tori and uke are in natural right-hand postures as tori walks backwards and draws uke forwards.

2 Tori withdraws his left leg and hip, adding power to the high pulling action applied to uke's sleeve as uke's balance is broken to his front right corner. Tori's right foot slides diagonally across to a spot on the outside edge of uke's advancing right foot.

3 Tori begins to pivot his right foot as he continu pulling around to his le the elbow of his bent r arm moving across the front of uke's chest, as morote-seoi-nage.

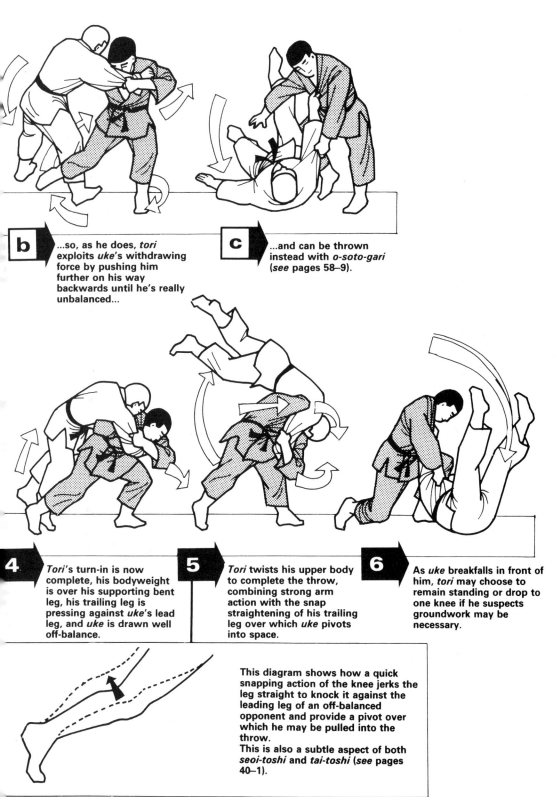

b ...so, as he does, *tori* exploits *uke*'s withdrawing force by pushing him further on his way backwards until he's really unbalanced...

c ...and can be thrown instead with *o-soto-gari* (*see* pages 58–9).

4 *Tori*'s turn-in is now complete, his bodyweight is over his supporting bent leg, his trailing leg is pressing against *uke*'s lead leg, and *uke* is drawn well off-balance.

5 *Tori* twists his upper body to complete the throw, combining strong arm action with the snap straightening of his trailing leg over which *uke* pivots into space.

6 As *uke* breakfalls in front of him, *tori* may choose to remain standing or drop to one knee if he suspects groundwork may be necessary.

This diagram shows how a quick snapping action of the knee jerks the leg straight to knock it against the leading leg of an off-balanced opponent and provide a pivot over which he may be pulled into the throw.

This is also a subtle aspect of both *seoi-toshi* and *tai-toshi* (*see* pages 40–1).

KATA-GURUMA Shoulder wheel

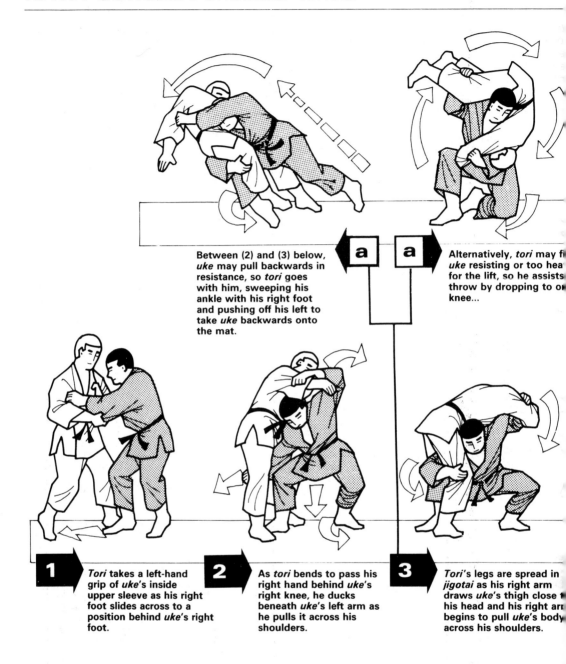

Between (2) and (3) below, *uke* may pull backwards in resistance, so *tori* goes with him, sweeping his ankle with his right foot and pushing off his left to take *uke* backwards onto the mat.

a **a**

Alternatively, *tori* may fi uke resisting or too hea for the lift, so he assists throw by dropping to o knee...

1 *Tori* takes a left-hand grip of *uke*'s inside upper sleeve as his right foot slides across to a position behind *uke*'s right foot.

2 As *tori* bends to pass his right hand behind *uke*'s right knee, he ducks beneath *uke*'s left arm as he pulls it across his shoulders.

3 *Tori*'s legs are spread in *jigotai* as his right arm draws *uke*'s thigh close t his head and his right arr begins to pull *uke*'s body across his shoulders.

ta-guruma is one of the more spectacular *judo* ows and it is not recommended that beginners empt it until they have (if *tori*) acquired the ength of *jigotai* from which to raise an op-nent upwards or (if *uke*) have become suffi- ciently proficient at *ukemi* to breakfall from what might be a height of 1½ metres (5 ft).

Jigotai is, of course, the widespread posture of defence on bent knees. However, bend too low and your lift-power will become impaired. Conversely, bend too little and it will be impossible to position yourself correctly for the implementation of the throw. Moving in and lifting, without completing the throw, is one aspect of *kata-guruma* you may practise without the need for your partner to be repeatedly breakfalling from height. Otherwise, the use of a crash-mat is advised, or a heavy bag could substitute for a partner. Anyway, you'll eventually discover the right degree of knee-bend from which to exert maximum lifting strength. Work on it!

Also, develop the art of rolling *uke* across the back of your shoulders as you are in the act of rising. That way, you'll discover that the full weight of *uke* has passed over one shoulder to begin dropping via its own momentum down the other side long before you've reached breaking point or risen fully to an upright posture. Attempt rising upright before you've begun rolling *uke* and you may have problems!

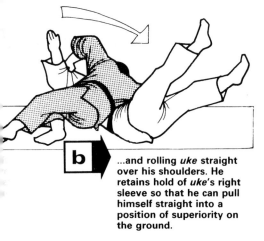

b ...and rolling *uke* straight over his shoulders. He retains hold of *uke*'s right sleeve so that he can pull himself straight into a position of superiority on the ground.

4 As *tori* rises upwards, he uses both arms to propel *uke* right across his shoulders, behind his neck.

5 By the time *tori* is as upright as he needs to be, *uke* has been pulled through the point of balance and drops down the other side.

6 *Tori* retains control with his left hand as his right pushes *uke* into final orbit, stepping back with his right foot to clear the landing area.

SUMI-OTOSHI Corner drop

Sumi-otoshi is another hand technique with no body contact being incurred during execution. However, it is the force of your twisting body, transmitted through the arms, which helps generate the real power to perform any *te-waza* effectively. *Sumi-otoshi*, whether applied from a standing or *sutemi-waza* (sacrifice technique) posture, is certainly no exception to this.

As with most throwing techniques, the amount of your own power required to execute *sumi-otoshi* can depend very much upon your timing of delivery combining with the extent to which you can exploit your opponent's advancing energy force. Choosing the critical moment for your attack is all important if you are to maximise the opportunity.

This theory may be best understood in relation to the rear dropping action of *tori* as he is shown going to ground in order to deliver the throw. Once taken off-balance to a front corner, the falling weight of *uke* alone is sufficient to generate at least some oncoming force, regardless of the rate at which he may have been moving forwards anyway before the attack was launched.

On the other hand, it is far more difficult to execute *sumi-toshi* from a standing posture. This is generally only possible when *tori* is a strong and experienced *judoka* able to sense and immediately react to an opponent's line of movement and application of energy forces.

1 *Tori* walks backwards, drawing *uke* towards him until he takes a longer step back to his left. He pulls hard and swivels his body to break *uke*'s balance to the right front corner.

2 As *uke* attempts to regain his balance by placing his advancing right foot forward, *tori* drops to the rear, thrusting his right leg between *uke*'s feet.

3 *Uke* continues to be pulled further off-balance as *tori* drops to the mat, spreadeagles his legs, pulls close in with his left hand and pushes with his right

Viewed from the other side can be seen the action of *tori*'s right hand grasping *uke*'s lapel and pushing out strongly in unison with the left arm pulling in close.

c *Tori*'s positive body movement and strong arm action combine to girate *uke* to the mat and complete *tori*'s *sumi-otoshi*.

b *Tori* pushes firmly off his back foot, strong body twist transmitting power to his arms as *uke* is propelled off balance.

a *Tori* feints to right, then steps to left as *uke* resists by pulling that way.

4 Continued momentum is maintained as *tori* pulls in vigorously with his left hand and pushes out and upwards with his right, so that *uke* is spun into the air.

5 *Tori* presses off his flat right foot, adding strength to his upper body twist in support of his arms, as *uke* spirals to land on his back.

This aerial view shows the position in which *uke* lands in relation to *tori*.

UKI-OTOSHI Floating drop

Perhaps more than any other throwing technique, *uki-otoshi* provides the perfect example of the principles of *judo* by controlling an advancing opponent's energy and converting it for use as a force against him.

Although not generally part of any fixed syllabus work, *uki-otoshi* is the first technique a student must demonstrate when performing *nage-no-kata*, during which he drops to one knee in order to execute the throw as demonstrated here. Categorised as *te-waza* (hand technique), *uke-otoshi* may be executed also from a standing posture.

Whether applied kneeling or standing, *uki-otoshi* demands from *tori* perfect timing and a powerful arm action. The technique is usually applied in a *randori* or contest situation when *uke* is advancing at some speed, with *tori* in controlled retreat and waiting for the split second he senses that his opponent may be most effectively drawn off balance and into the throw.

a Instead of preparing to drop backwards and dow[n] to his left knee at this point, *tori* may swing his left foot to the rear...

1 In a normal right-hand posture, *uke* is advancing strongly towards *tori* who encourages him to come forwards.

2 Confident of *uke*'s momentum, *tori* takes an overhand reverse grip to pull on *uke*'s right sleeve and drops backwards onto his left knee.

3 *Uke* becomes unbalanced as *tori* completes his knee drop to the rear and out o[f] line with the spot upon which *uke* will eventually land.

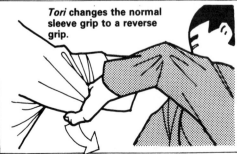

Tori changes the normal sleeve grip to a reverse grip.

Strong, revolving arm actions are essential to the execution of *uki-otoshi*, whether performed from a kneeling or standing posture.

b ▶ ...in order to pivot his body strongly to the left in support of strong arm action as *uke* is drawn off balance...

c ▶ ...to be propelled through the air in a floating movement which *uki-otoshi* executed from a standing posture.

d ▶ *Uke* breakfalls under the control of *tori* who is well positioned to go into groundwork if necessary.

4 ▶ In one continuous action, *tori* controls *uke*'s float through the air, pulling down vigorously with his left hand towards his own left hip and pushing strongly with his right.

5 ▶ *Uke* lands to the rear left corner of *tori* who finishes in classical posture, with his head up and facing forward and controlling *uke*'s right arm firmly with both hands.

HIZA-GURUMA Knee wheel

If there's a mistake most beginners are prone to make with o-soto-gari (see pages 58–9) it's attempting the attack so far out that there's no chance of reaching an opponent's legs, let alone taking him off balance to complete the throw.

The exact opposite might be said of hiza-guruma, for a fairly common mistake is to attempt the technique when too close in to an opponent. That way, the attacker is likely to become unbalanced, as well as being unable to provide the strong long-range pivoting action against an opponent's leg.

Tori must be far enough away from his opponent, arms only slightly bent, to permit room for the long and powerful sweeping action of the attacking leg as the sole of the foot turns in firmly to provide a pivot point against the outside of uke's knee. There must also be enough room between the opponents for tori to operate a strong, revolving arm action.

As tori rotates his arms to spiral uke over the point of the pivot, it sometimes helps to lean slightly backwards so that the body is in line with the outstretched attacking leg. Leaning back into this posture, whilst rotating the arms, is a movement a judoka can rehearse repeatedly on his own, without the need for a partner.

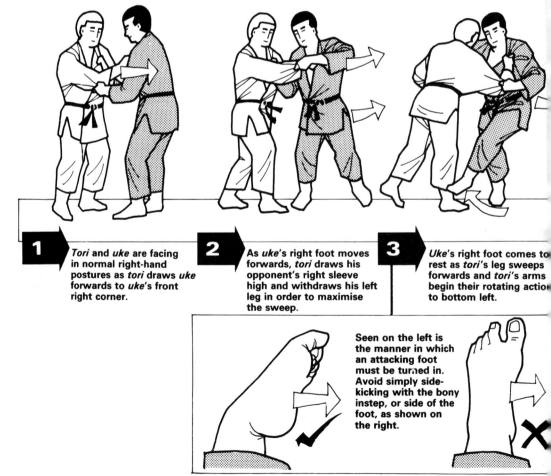

1 Tori and uke are facing in normal right-hand postures as tori draws uke forwards to uke's front right corner.

2 As uke's right foot moves forwards, tori draws his opponent's right sleeve high and withdraws his left leg in order to maximise the sweep.

3 Uke's right foot comes to rest as tori's leg sweeps forwards and tori's arms begin their rotating action to bottom left.

Seen on the left is the manner in which an attacking foot must be turned in. Avoid simply side-kicking with the bony instep, or side of the foot, as shown on the right.

a At this point, *uke* may have already managed to shift his full weight over his right leg and be able to resist, or block, *tori*'s knee-wheeling action.

b *Tori* feints again quickly to his left and as *uke* reacts towards *tori*'s right...

c *tori* changes his force direction and attacks to the right with his right leg outstretched to take *uke* over to the opposite side with the same *hiza-guruma* technique.

4 *Uke* now becomes fully off balance as *tori*'s left foot makes full contact with his right knee and *tori*'s arms continue rotating.

5 *Uke* is wheeled over *tori*'s foot as *tori* leans slightly back, pulling his left hand close into his hip and pushing out with his arm.

6 *Uke*'s wheel through the air continues until he breakfalls at the feet of *uke* who remains in control, ready for groundwork.

Shown here is *tori*'s steering wheel arm action as *uke* is wheeled through the air. *Tori*'s left arm circles down towards his left hip while the right arm extends slightly to help the spiralling movement of the 'wheel'.

O-UCHI-GARI Major inner reaping

O-uchi-gari is a useful technique to develop and perfect, because it may be used effectively in so many different situations, from either right or left side, as an attack in its own right or as part of most sequences of combination techniques.

A close-range technique, its most common usage is perhaps when an opponent has adopted a defensive posture, with either leg slightly advanced forward, or he leaves a leg forward while moving backwards in retreat.

When delivering *o-uchi-gari*, it's sometimes unavoidable that *tori* falls forwards on top of an opponent and is thereby committed to on-going groundwork. The chances of this happening may be minimised by practising the foot movements shown below. The back foot from which *tori* drives off is positioned behind the striking foot to form a 'T' and is at right angles to the direction of the throw. This simple movement adds thrusting power to *tori*'s attack, as well as helping to preserve balance. Any *judoka* can practise these sliding in and out foot movements by himself by placing a pair of trainers on the spots where an imaginary opponent's feet might be.

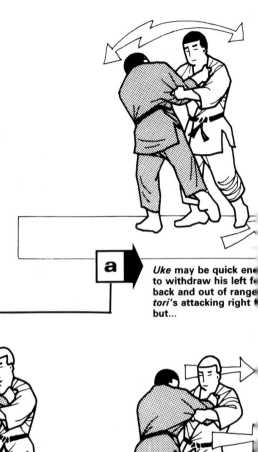

a *Uke* may be quick enough to withdraw his left foot back and out of range of *tori*'s attacking right but...

1 *Tori* and *uke* are facing each other in natural right-hand postures as *uke* begins to retreat with his right foot, leaving the left foot slightly forward.

2 *Tori* pushes, simultaneously swivelling his left foot square to the line of attack and driving off it to slip his right leg between *uke*'s.

3 Maintaining his forward drive, *tori* turns his right leg in a circular movement so that his knee is immediately behind *uke*'s left knee.

Shown on the right is the sequence of foot movements as *tori* brings his left foot up behind his right, swivels them into a 'T'-formation and then slides the right foot forwards between *uke*'s feet.

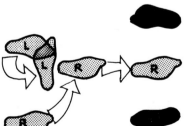

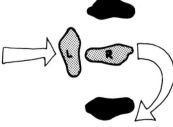

b ► ...this leaves *uke*'s right leg forward and exposed to a follow-through attack by *tori*...

c ► ...who sweeps the same attacking right leg across his front and behind *uke*'s right leg...

d ► ...to throw *uke* backwards with an alternative, or combination, *kouchi-gari* (*see* pages 64–5).

4 ► Continuing to drive off the back foot, *tori* sweeps his right leg towards his own rear right corner, sliding it along the inside of *uke*'s left leg to clip the back of *uke*'s heel and taking him totally off balance to his rear.

5 ► *Tori* follows right through with his drive forwards as his leg sweep is completed and he attempts to retain his own balance.

6 ► Having failed to retain his balance, *tori* continues forwards to trap *uke*'s inner thigh with his knee and clear his way through into a continuing groundwork attack.

O-SOTO-GARI Major outer reaping

The sad thing about *o-soto-gari* is that, unless curbed and corrected by a conscientious *sensei*, it can become little more than a lazy beginner's bad habit. The attraction is, of course, that it does not require turning-in effort or great energy or body contact, such as is demanded by any of the major hip techniques. What is more, even a badly performed *o-soto-gari* has been known to yield a result.

However, the student *judoka* should be able to avoid all long-range 'hacking' efforts from the outset by studying all the elements of *o-soto-gari* and rehearsing the technique in slow motion. From that will come an understanding of what the technique really is and why it works so beautifully when applied properly under the right circumstances.

Once perfected, *o-soto-gari* is a clean, crisp and powerful throwing technique which is adaptable for use in many situations as a counter throw or to be worked into combination sequences. It's especially useful as a counter against an opponent caught mid-way between turning in, or out, to left or right sides, or against one who is moving forwards towards you with some force.

a At this point, *uke* has resisted *tori*'s attack w spiralling hop to his le taking his weight over left foot.

1 As *uke*'s right foot is advanced, *tori* steps well forwards with his left, to take *uke* off balance to his rear right corner.

2 *Tori* pulls hard down on *uke*'s left sleeve while pushing with his right arm and threading his right foot through.

3 *Uke* is already beginnin spiral as *tori* continues forward drive, straighte his right leg out behind and preparing to reap.

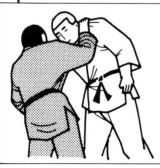

To assist in breaking *uke*'s balance to his rear right corner, *tori* may choose a high grip on the side of *uke*'s collar, pressing his forearm against the side of *uke*'s neck to help force him sideways.

Alternatively, maintaining a normal lapel grip, *tori* may opt simply to curl his fist and drive across *uke*.

b ▶ *Tori* exploits this situation by transposing his intended *osoto-gari* leg sweep into a sweep up high against *uke*'s top inner thigh...

c ▶ ...pivoting on his left foot and drawing *uke* forwards to throw him with *uchi-mata* (*see* pages 66–7)...

d ▶ ...and then, as always, maintaining control of his opponent in readiness to drop straightaway into groundwork.

4 ▶ *Tori*'s strong arm action supports the power of his reaping leg as it straightens and sweeps high behind *uke*'s thigh.

5 ▶ *Tori*'s sweeping leg and dipping head are in line as he leans forwards to continue the throw and *uke* is rolled off the back of his thigh.

6 ▶ *Tori* regains balance on both feet as *uke* is pulled through towards a breakfall.

As always with a sweeping leg, it is safer to curl in the toes of the foot even though, as in *o-soto-gari*, the actual foot never (or should never) makes contact with an opponent.

SASAE-TSURI-KOMI-ASHI Propping drawing ankle

Sasae-tsuri-komi-ashi is sometimes translated as 'the lifting pull throw with supporting foot' and, except for the omission of the word 'propping', it is perhaps more fully descriptive of what happens in the course of executing the technique.

The student must remember that the movement of the attacking foot is not a powerful sweep, but more a very firmly delivered clip. The curled-in sole of the foot is against an opponent's ankle, thereby providing a low fulcrum pivot over which *uke* is tipped off balance.

The 1961 World Champion, Dutchman Anton Geesink, was reputedly known for the excellence of his *sasae-tsuri-komi-ashi*. Further back than that, history (legend?) tells us of Yoshiaki Yamashita (10th Dan) who, in the early 1890s shortly after the establishment of the Kodokan, organised a world-wide *jujutsu* meeting at the Japanese Police Ministry and astounded everyone with the supremacy he achieved by use of his allegedly superb *sasae-tsuri-komi-ashi*.

a Here's where *uke* ma resist and attempt to regain balance by ste forwards and changi weight onto his left f

1 Tori faces *uke*; both are in natural right-hand postures as *tori* begins to open his left side by stepping to the rear with his left foot.

2 Tori simultaneously pulls *uke*'s right sleeve and *uke* steps forwards onto his right foot in an attempt to regain balance.

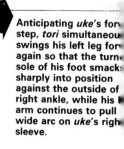

3 Anticipating *uke*'s for step, *tori* simultaneou swings his left leg for again so that the turn sole of his foot smack sharply into position against the outside of right ankle, while his arm continues to pull wide arc on *uke*'s righ sleeve.

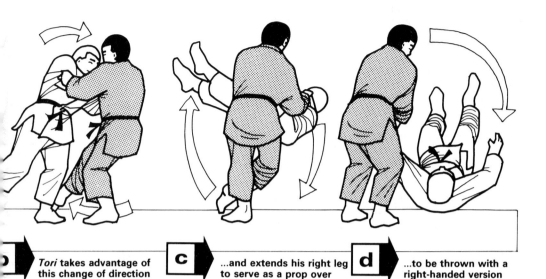

b ▶ *Tori* takes advantage of this change of direction to *uke*'s momentum...

c ▶ ...and extends his right leg to serve as a prop over which *uke* is pulled...

d ▶ ...to be thrown with a right-handed version of the same *sasae-tsuri-komi-ashi*.

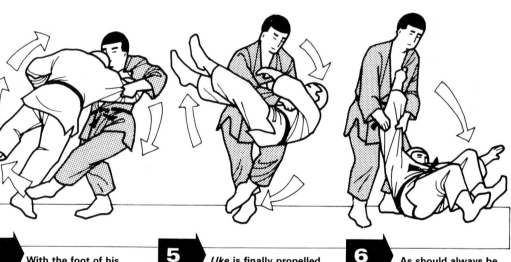

▶ With the foot of his extended left leg providing a low fulcrum, *tori* directs his left-arm pull towards his own left hip, pushing across on *uke*'s left lapel with his right hand so that *uke* is taken completely off balance to his right side.

5 ▶ *Uke* is finally propelled through the air and turned onto his back by the circular pulling action of *tori*'s arms.

This shows the simultaneous movements of *tori*'s propping foot and the steering wheel arm action while an upright and well-balanced stance is maintained – something else you can practise and perfect without the need for a partner!

6 ▶ As should always be the case, *tori* retains control as *uke* breakfalls to the mat.

DEASHI-BARAI Advancing foot sweep

Apart from *tori*'s perfect timing, little else is required to make a success of this subtle but devastating technique. Perhaps no one can look more surprised (or annoyed!) than the person who has just been caught with a point-scoring *deashi-barai*.

Tori's correct timing is focused upon the critical moment at which an opponent's leading foot has come forwards to settle on the mat, but has not yet taken upon it the full weight of the rest of the body. Before that can happen, at the critical moment when the foot first settles on the mat *tori* must skim the outside edge of his attacking foot across the mat to strike with the inside of the curled-in sole against the outside of *uke*'s ankle.

The sweeping movement of the leg is synchronised with the steering wheel action of *tori*'s arms, a combination of movements which a *judoka* may practise alone without a partner (*see sasae-tsuri-komi-ashi, pages 60–1*).

Practise all foot and leg techniques with a partner at, say, three-quarter speed to discover the distance you need between you in order to work the legs while at the same time leaving space for effective arm actions.

a At this point, *uke* foil *tori*'s attack by withdrawing his left and pulling away to side as he does so.

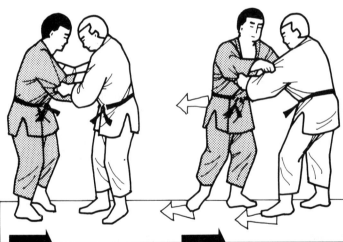

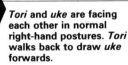

1 *Tori* and *uke* are facing each other in normal right-hand postures. *Tori* walks back to draw *uke* forwards.

2 As *tori* opens his right side by withdrawing his right leg to add strength to his pull, *tori* changes his normal lapel grip to pull on the outside top of *uke*'s left sleeve.
This change of grip will give him a greater purchase for his pull as he moves further into the attack, breaking *uke*'s balance to the front left corner and forcing him to attempt to regain balance by bringing his left foot forwards.

3 Just before *uke* tran his weight fully onto advancing left foot, anticipated the mov has swept the right forwards again, skin the mat to strike the outside of *uke*'s ankl the curled-in sole of foot. While the foot through and up, *tori* action revolves arou down in the opposit direction.

b ▶ *Tori* follows *uke*'s new line of momentum and switches to a left-footed sweep against *uke*'s right leg...

c ▶ ...combining it with a circular arm action towards *uke*'s right side and...

d ▶ ...having switched to a left-handed *deashi-barai* in which he turns *uke* over towards a breakfall in front of him.

4 ▶ The sweeping foot does not simply provide a 'prop', as in *sasae-tsuri-komi-ashi*, but is carried through across the front of *tori*'s supporting leg.

5 ▶ *Tori*'s arm action rolls *uke* over in mid-air so his back is towards the breakfall.

6 ▶ *Tori* fully controls *uke* as his opponent lands across the front of his feet.

In a low-sweeping foot movement, during which the foot is literally skimmed across the surface of the mat, the curling-in of the toes not only speeds up the delivery but helps prevent injury to the attacker's toes.

KOUCHI-GARI Small inner reap

Performed skilfully, *kouchi-gari* can be a subtle but effective technique which, with practice, can be usefully executed at close quarters to either right or left sides without the need necessarily to change your grip on your opponent and telegraph your intentions.

Probably the greatest problem is that of *tori* maintaining his balance during the execution of this technique and this is particularly so for beginners. Fortunately, the footwork which helps to avoid this may be practised independently, without a partner.

Practise sliding backwards and forwards, with your lead foot pointing to the front. Bring your back foot close up to the lead foot, placing it sideways and pointing outwards against the back of the lead foot heel to form a letter 'T'. Until this stage, the movements are similar to those illustrated for the foot movements of *o-uchi-gari* on pages 56–7.

From this point, push off the back foot as you slide the lead foot in a scooping movement across the front of you towards the point where your opponent's diagonally opposite foot might be.

a At this point, *uke* may anticipated *tori*'s foot sweep and he withdraw his left foot backwards out of range.

1 *Tori*, for the purpose of clarity of this demonstration, has taken a left-handed grip and prepares to draw *uke* forwards.

2 *Tori* withdraws his right hip to assist in breaking *uke*'s balance to front left corner as he pulls on *uke*'s left sleeve.

3 *Tori* drives off his back foot, pushing forwards extending his left leg across the front towar *uke*'s left heel.

b ▶ But, as *uke* re-settles with his right foot forward, *tori* halts his withdrawal and pushes forwards again to sustain his attack...

c ▶ ...by reaching forwards with his extended left leg towards the inside of *uke*'s right leg...

d ▶ ...and taking him backwards with *o-uchi-gari* (*see* pages 56–7).

4 ▶ *Tori* continues pushing forwards, sweeping his curled-in foot across the mat until the sole clips the back of *uke*'s left heel.

5 ▶ *Uke* is completely unbalanced and falls to the rear as *tori* continues, at the same time regaining his own balance...

6 ▶ ...or following through immediately, if necessary, into groundwork.

Note especially how *tori*'s foot curls inwards as it skims across the mat, so that the actual impact against *uke*'s heel is made with the sole of the foot and not the bony instep.

UCHI-MATA Inner thigh reap

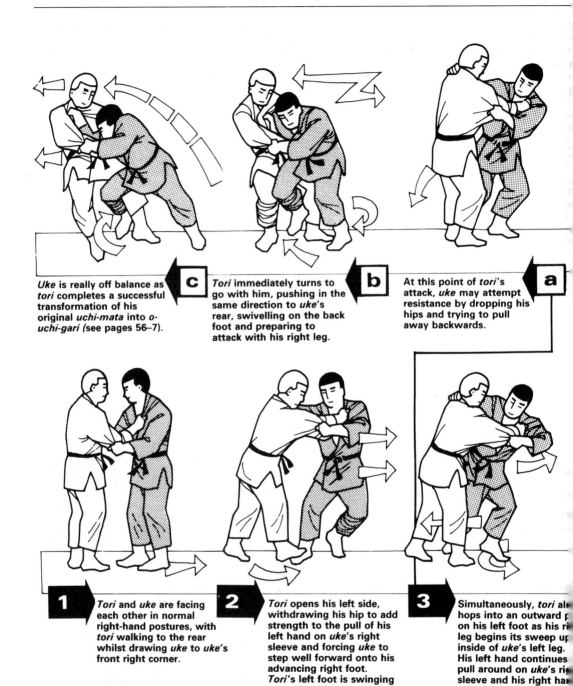

c *Uke* is really off balance as *tori* completes a successful transformation of his original *uchi-mata* (see pages 56–7).

b *Tori* immediately turns to go with him, pushing in the same direction to *uke*'s rear, swivelling on the back foot and preparing to attack with his right leg.

a At this point of *tori*'s attack, *uke* may attempt resistance by dropping his hips and trying to pull away backwards.

1 *Tori* and *uke* are facing each other in normal right-hand postures, with *tori* walking to the rear whilst drawing *uke* to *uke*'s front right corner.

2 *Tori* opens his left side, withdrawing his hip to add strength to the pull of his left hand on *uke*'s right sleeve and forcing *uke* to step well forward onto his advancing right foot. *Tori*'s left foot is swinging around to his own rear left corner.

3 Simultaneously, *tori* al... hops into an outward p... on his left foot as his ri... leg begins its sweep up... inside of *uke*'s left leg. His left hand continues... pull around on *uke*'s ri... sleeve and his right ha... grips high behind *uke*'s collar in order to pull h... forwards and upwards against his body.

good *uchi-mata* can be a match winner in any
competitive situation, which is why it ranks high
in the repertoire of most contest men and senior
players who have acquired the maturity of
strength and timing required to execute the technique properly.

It is also a major technique with many recognised variations from which players can select the
one which suits their own particular physique or
style of *judo*.

Common to all variations of *uchi-mata*, though,
is the need to step in deeply initially and to draw
your opponent well in towards you when turning
in to make the powerful leg sweep. To turn and
sweep from too far out will make the attack totally
ineffective and possibly very dangerous, as a
long-range leg sweep can easily finish up as a
harmful kick into your opponent's crutch.

One of the most difficult aspects to master of
any *uchi-mata* is the art of almost hopping around
as you swivel into attack, turning your supporting
foot as you do so to point in the direction of the
throw which thereby helps you to maintain your
balance. Variations of *uchi-mata* include changes
to the right-hand grip and the point at which *tori*'s
sweeping leg strikes *uke*'s inner thigh. Shown
here is the recognised basic *uchi-mata*.

4 *Tori* twists his upper body down towards his left, pulls through with his arms and reaps his right leg up against *uke*'s inner thigh.

5 As *tori*'s leg reaches its highest point, his upper body has dipped well forward and down, and has twisted to his left.

6 *Uke* is rolled off the top of the back of *tori*'s thigh. *Tori* retains his balance as his left arm pulls through on his opponent's right sleeve which he continues to control as *uke* breakfalls to the mat.

Tori demonstrates the point at which his attacking leg will begin moving in against *uke*'s inner thigh, though he will of course be much deeper in at the moment of attack (*see* fig. 4 above).

O-SOTO-GURUMA Large outer wheel

The obvious difference between *o-soto-guruma* and *o-soto-gari* (*see* pages 58–9) is that in order to execute the former it is necessary for *tori* to step in much deeper around his opponent's near-leg than for the latter in order that he can reach across to reap away both of *uke*'s legs (not a single leg as in *o-soto-gari*).

For this same reason, it is a throw seldom used with any success as an isolated direct attack during competition *judo*. Few experienced players would allow an opponent sufficient space in which to move around as deeply as the attacker must in order to perform the two-legged reap.

On the other hand, beginners more often manage *o-soto-guruma* almost by default when competing among themselves, but only because they've gone in too wildly for *o-soto-gari* and have accidentally gathered both legs into their reaping action.

However, *o-soto-guruma* must not be underrated, particularly as a counter throw used at the critical moment when an opponent is turning in (or out!) of his attack. Also, practise *o-soto-guruma* as a follow-through to an *o-soto-gari* which your opponent has tried to avoid by moving his near-side leg forwards. Don't retreat, but attack again to sweep his far leg as well with *o-soto-guruma*.

a This is when *uke* may p[ush] back to resist *tori*'s oso[to]-*guruma* attack, so *tori* feints as though to turn out, but immediately attacks again vigorousl[y]

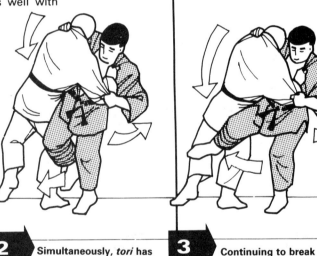

1 *Tori* breaks *uke*'s balance to *uke*'s rear right corner, assisting this by taking a high grip on *uke*'s left collar and forcing his forearm against the side of his opponent's neck, while pulling downwards and forwards with his left hand on *uke*'s right sleeve.

2 Simultaneously, *tori* has stepped well forward with his left foot alongside *uke*'s right, forcing his own bodyweight forward over his supporting left leg and threading his right leg high between himself and his opponent.

3 Continuing to break *uk[e's]* balance to the rear righ[t] corner, *tori* has now dr[iven] his right leg completely through, beginning alre[ady] to twist his upper body [to] his left as the back of h[is] right thigh makes cont[act] with the top of the bac[k of] *uke*'s right thigh. The l[eft] reaping action of *tori*'s right leg should stretch diagonally from the rea[r] top of *uke*'s near thigh [to] the rear calf of *uke*'s fa[r] leg. It is struck with the sole of *tori*'s curled-in, pointed foot.

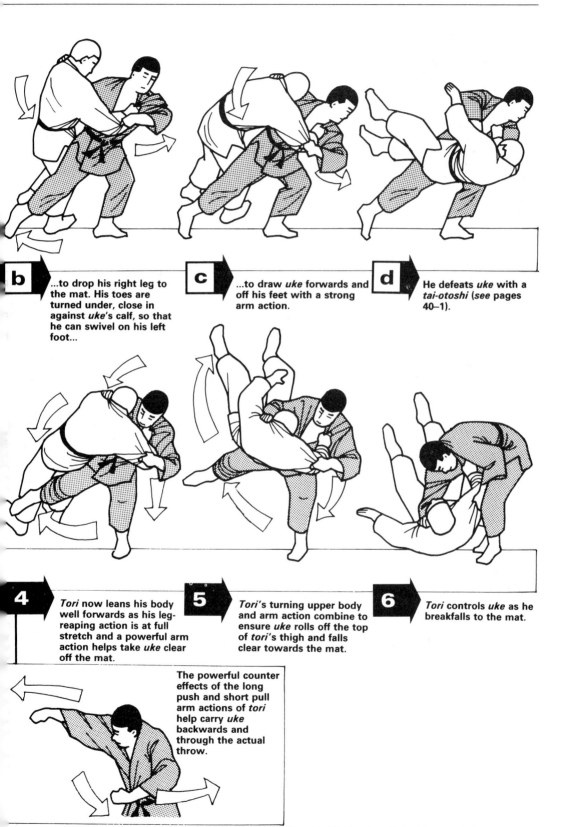

b ...to drop his right leg to the mat. His toes are turned under, close in against *uke*'s calf, so that he can swivel on his left foot...

c ...to draw *uke* forwards and off his feet with a strong arm action.

d He defeats *uke* with a *tai-otoshi* (*see* pages 40–1).

4 *Tori* now leans his body well forwards as his leg-reaping action is at full stretch and a powerful arm action helps take *uke* clear off the mat.

5 *Tori*'s turning upper body and arm action combine to ensure *uke* rolls off the top of *tori*'s thigh and falls clear towards the mat.

6 *Tori* controls *uke* as he breakfalls to the mat.

The powerful counter effects of the long push and short pull arm actions of *tori* help carry *uke* backwards and through the actual throw.

KOSOTO-GARI Minor outer reap

Like some other foot techniques, *kosoto-gari* can be sweet, simple and surprisingly effective if applied by the *judoka* who keeps cool in the face of, for example, a frenzied attack by an over-energetic opponent. It can also be useful against an opponent who fails to complete a technique and then steps out of his line of balance to leave himself vulnerable to a counter technique.

The swift, neat action of *kosoto-gari* requires the support of strong and fast arm actions in order to take *uke* over into the air and control his fall to the mat. It's a real opportunist technique which *tori* must slip into at the critical moment *uke* shows himself to be potentially vulnerable. For that reason, it's a relatively close-quarter technique, leaving *uke* with little or preferably no indication of what is coming.

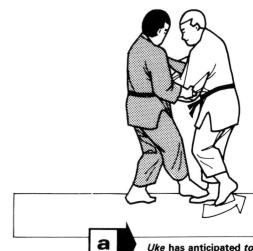

a *Uke* has anticipated to intentions and he quick foils the attack by sim withdrawing his left fo backwards, out of distance...

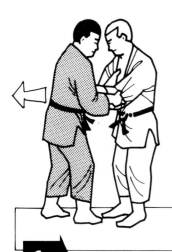

1 For the purpose of clear demonstration, *tori* and *uke* are facing each other in left-hand postures with normal sleeve and lapel grips.
Tori draws *uke* forwards, at the same time stepping backwards so that his rear foot comes slightly round to his rear left, taking him to the left side of *uke*'s central line of approach.

2 Simultaneously, *tori* pulls on *uke*'s left sleeve and *uke* is forced to step forwards with his left foot to correct balance.
Tori immediately skims his right foot, sole facing in with toes curled under, over the mat towards *uke*'s advanced foot.

3 The sole of *tori*'s curle foot strikes solidly agai the rear outside of *uke* left heel as his arm act begins.

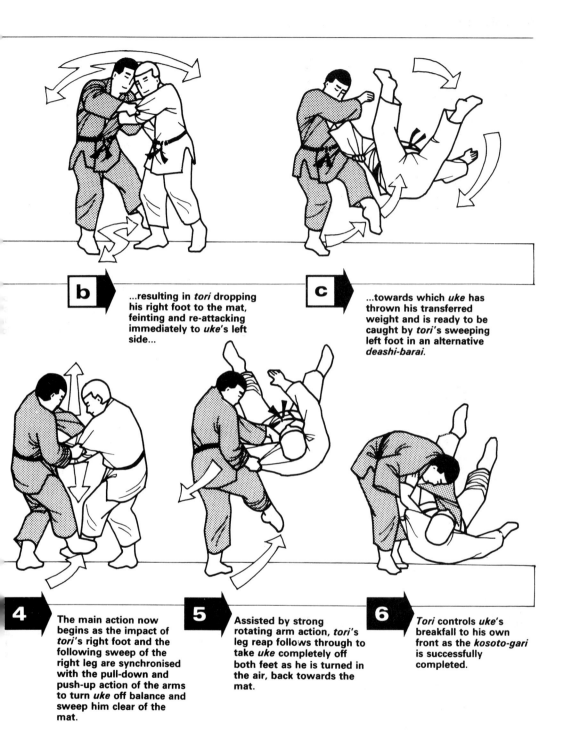

b ...resulting in *tori* dropping his right foot to the mat, feinting and re-attacking immediately to *uke*'s left side...

c ...towards which *uke* has thrown his transferred weight and is ready to be caught by *tori*'s sweeping left foot in an alternative *deashi-barai*.

4 The main action now begins as the impact of *tori*'s right foot and the following sweep of the right leg are synchronised with the pull-down and push-up action of the arms to turn *uke* off balance and sweep him clear of the mat.

5 Assisted by strong rotating arm action, *tori*'s leg reap follows through to take *uke* completely off both feet as he is turned in the air, back towards the mat.

6 *Tori* controls *uke*'s breakfall to his own front as the *kosoto-gari* is successfully completed.

KOSOTO-GAKE Small outer hook

Gake means 'hooking action'. *Kosote-gake* means a small outer hook, as opposed to *kosoto-gari* which is a small or minor outer reap. *Kosoto-gake* was once considered to be no more than a variation of *kosoto-gari*, but it is now regarded as a technique in its own right.

And so it should be, if one story is correct which attributes the creation of *kosoto-gake* to one Hidekazu Nagaoka who eventually became a high-ranking Kodokan Dan grade. It is said that Nagaoka studied from childhood with a Kito *jujutsu* group, practising in the fields surrounding his Okayama village home. In 1915, he left his village, travelled to Tokyo and took up the study of Kodokan *judo*. He found himself at a loss to

cope immediately with adapting his form | unarmed combat to that of Kodokan *jud* students. Desperate to succeed, he spent mar days studying the others in training. What he sav he analysed, considered and out came a tecl nique we call *kosoto-gake*.

As with all foot and leg techniques, practise th movement in slow motion in order to estima your best attacking range. Attack from too far o and your intentions will be telegraphed to you opponent (and your leg actions will be ineffectiv anyway). Attack from too near in and there won be sufficient space between you and your partn to execute the powerful circular throwing actio of the arms.

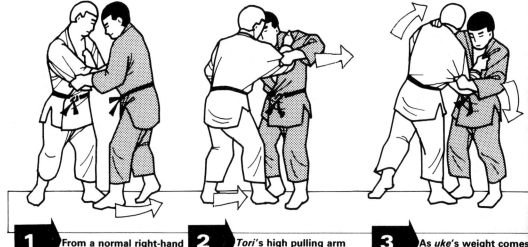

1 From a normal right-hand posture, *tori* pulls *uke* forwards, withdrawing his left leg and opening up his left side to add power to the action.

2 *Tori's* high pulling arm action takes *uke* off balance to his front right corner and he's forced to step his right foot forwards to correct the imbalance.

3 As *uke's* weight comes over his supporting rigl leg, *tori* transfers his rig lapel grip to one high o *uke's* side collar so that he can push and simultaneously pull to t right with his left-hand on *uke's* sleeve.

a *Uke* resists *tori*'s attack and attempts to regain his balance by swinging his left foot round to place it firmly down to his left side...

b ...but before he can complete his turn, *tori* pulls on *uke*'s right sleeve and pushes with his right forearm against the side of *uke*'s collar.

c The result is that *uke* is completely off balance as *tori* threads his sweeping leg through, and turns his upper body to his left to reap and throw *uke* with *o-soto-gari* (*see* pages 58–9).

4 As this strong, synchronised arm action drives towards *uke*'s rear right corner, *tori*'s left leg is extended. His toes are pointed to hook around the calf of *uke*'s right leg.

5 *Tori*'s left leg hooks around the back of *uke*'s calf to carry it across the front of his own supporting leg.

6 The speed of the hook, combined with the revolving arm action, carries both of *uke*'s feet clear of the mat as *tori* drops his left foot to retain his balance and control *uke*'s breakfall.

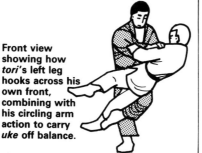

Front view showing how *tori*'s left leg hooks across his own front, combining with his circling arm action to carry *uke* off balance.

O-GURUMA Major wheel

O-guruma has similarities with another throwing technique called *ashi-guruma* (leg wheel). In both techniques, *tori*'s rear leg sweeps backwards to provide a prop over which *uke* is drawn and then pivoted into the throw. The main difference between the techniques is the height at which *tori*'s sweeping leg makes contact with *uke*.

Similar in principle to both techniques is *hiza-guruma* (*see* pages 54–5), but in the execution of this, the foot of *tori*'s extended prop makes contact lower down still with the outside of *uke*'s knee.

At first glance, any beginner might also confuse o-guruma with *harai-goshi* (*see* pages 28–9), but in the latter it is the final twist of the hips, and not the sweep or propping value of the leg itself, which throws *uke* off the back top of *tori*'s thigh.

a Uke may attempt resistance at this point dropping his hips to lo his centre of gravity...

1 Tori and *uke* are facing each other, having taken normal right-handed grips of each other's opposite sleeves and lapels.
Tori steps well back with his left foot to open his left side and add strength to his pulling power on *uke*'s right arm.

2 As *tori* draws *uke* off balance to *uke*'s front right corner, he pivots on his left foot and slides his right hand up to grip the rear left of *uke*'s collar.

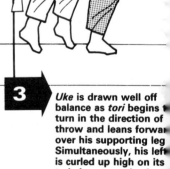

3 Uke is drawn well off balance as *tori* begins t turn in the direction of throw and leans forwar over his supporting leg Simultaneously, his lef is curled up high on its to being swept backwa against *uke*'s front top thigh, or even his lowe abdomen.

b ...so *tori* instantly attacks lower still, swinging his right arm forwards across *uke*'s front...

c ...to propel himself instead into a powerful *makikomi* attack (*see* pages 96–7).

4 Now fully turned, with sweeping leg at full stretch, *tori* pulls to pivot *uke* into the throw.

5 *Uke* is pulled fully towards his front right corner as he pivots over *tori*'s extended leg.

6 *Tori*'s strong arm action controls *uke* throughout, ensuring that he's turned over in flight to breakfall on his back in a position from which *tori* can easily drop into groundwork.

Diagram shows the approximate heights at which *tori*'s sweeping leg makes contact with *uke*.

– O-GURUMA

– ASHI-GURUMA

OKURI-ASHI-BARAI Side sweeping ankle throw

Okuri-ashi-barai is an attacking foot sweep directed against an opponent's foot but which, if timed correctly, should have a knock-on effect and take both of his feet up into the air.

The timing of *okuri-ashi-barai* is a critical factor in the execution of this throw, but get it right and you'll be capable of dealing with opponents much heavier than yourself. The critical moment to strike *uke*'s foot is the instant his bodyweight has passed over its point of vertical balance and is *about* to come down upon the foot which is to be swept.

As a foot sweep, it differs from *deashi-barai* (see pages 62–3) mainly in that it takes an opponent off balance sideways, rather than first being drawn to a front corner.

Okuri-ashi-barai is a *Nage-no-kata* technique and during *kata* it must be performed to both left and right sides, taking an appropriately specified number of sideways steps before executing the throw (see 'About kata' on page 96).

a If *tori*'s not quick eno⟨ here's when *uke* may what's happening an⟨ withdraw his right fo⟨ back out of range...

1 *Tori* and *uke* are facing each other, both having taken normal right-hand grips on opposite sleeves and lapels as they walk sideways in step with eac other in *tsugi-ashi* (see page 14).

2 *Tori* then takes an extra long step to his right.

3 Then, as *uke*'s right f⟨ slides to a halt *tori* sw with his left foot.

Again, the toes curl under and the attacking foot is turned inwards so that it's the soft undersole of *tori*'s foot that strikes the bony outside of *uke*'s foot or ankle.

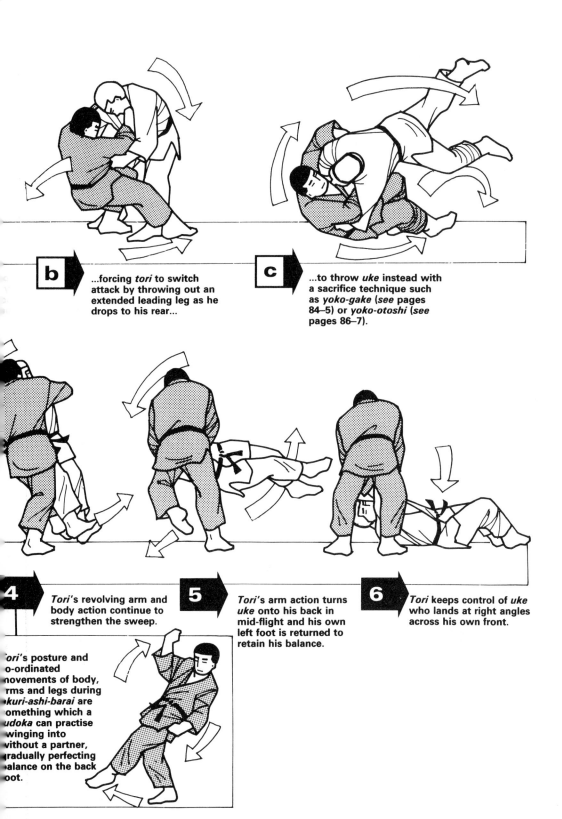

b ...forcing *tori* to switch attack by throwing out an extended leading leg as he drops to his rear...

c ...to throw *uke* instead with a sacrifice technique such as *yoko-gake* (*see* pages 84–5) or *yoko-otoshi* (*see* pages 86–7).

4 *Tori*'s revolving arm and body action continue to strengthen the sweep.

5 *Tori*'s arm action turns *uke* onto his back in mid-flight and his own left foot is returned to retain his balance.

6 *Tori* keeps control of *uke* who lands at right angles across his own front.

Tori's posture and co-ordinated movements of body, arms and legs during *okuri-ashi-barai* are something which a *judoka* can practise swinging into without a partner, gradually perfecting balance on the back foot.

TOMOE-NAGE Stomach throw

Tomoe-nage is a spectacular throw to which all beginners aspire, but they should not be allowed to attempt it (or have it tried on them) until they have achieved certain basic proficiencies.

To be taught this throw, *tori* must be experienced enough to be able to control his own body movements in the heat of action and be able to place the foot of his lifting leg accurately and precisely against the correct part of *uke*'s body, thereby avoiding the likelihood of unnecessary injury. *Tori* must also have acquired the confidence to step into his opponent deeply and without hesitation, committing himself fully and freely to the execution of the technique.

As with any *sutemi-waza*, he who hesitates is more often than not lost. Apart from the possibility of injury to either *judoka* as a result of a sloppily performed *tomoe-nage*, a failed technique might too easily result in *tori* becoming involved in groundwork it would have been well to avoid. In fact, unless a player becomes so proficient at *tomoe-nage* that a full *ippon* (ten-point winning score) or a *wazari* (seven points) is almost guaranteed, *tomoe-nage* is not the throw in contest terms for anyone with any doubts about their groundwork ability.

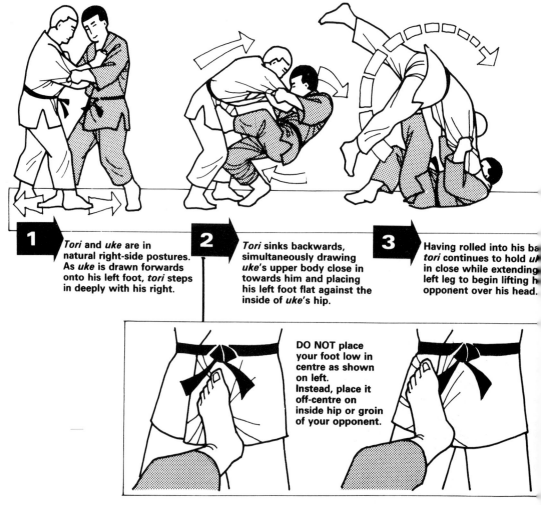

1 Tori and *uke* are in natural right-side postures. As *uke* is drawn forwards onto his left foot, *tori* steps in deeply with his right.

2 *Tori* sinks backwards, simultaneously drawing *uke*'s upper body close in towards him and placing his left foot flat against the inside of *uke*'s hip.

3 Having rolled into his ba *tori* continues to hold *uk* in close while extending left leg to begin lifting h opponent over his head.

DO NOT place your foot low in centre as shown on left. Instead, place it off-centre on inside hip or groin of your opponent.

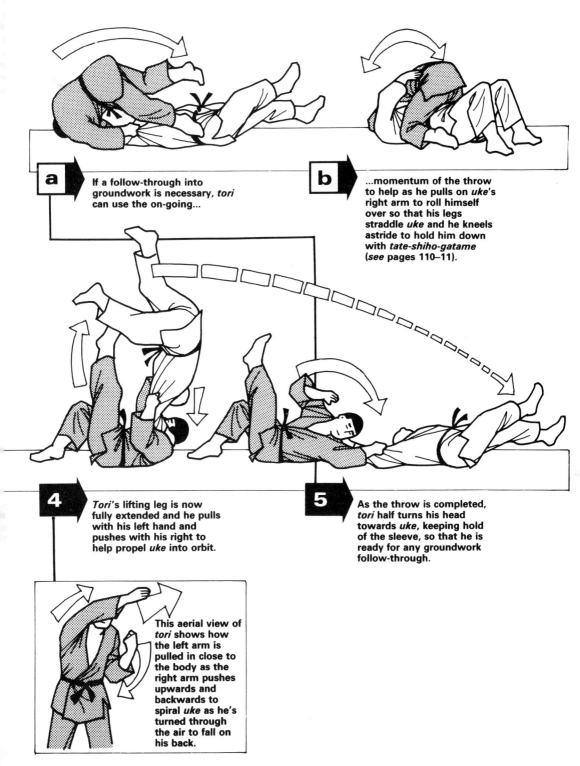

a If a follow-through into groundwork is necessary, *tori* can use the on-going...

b ...momentum of the throw to help as he pulls on *uke*'s right arm to roll himself over so that his legs straddle *uke* and he kneels astride to hold him down with *tate-shiho-gatame* (*see* pages 110–11).

4 *Tori*'s lifting leg is now fully extended and he pulls with his left hand and pushes with his right to help propel *uke* into orbit.

5 As the throw is completed, *tori* half turns his head towards *uke*, keeping hold of the sleeve, so that he is ready for any groundwork follow-through.

This aerial view of *tori* shows how the left arm is pulled in close to the body as the right arm pushes upwards and backwards to spiral *uke* as he's turned through the air to fall on his back.

URA-NAGE Rear throw

Ura-nage is a useful block or counter technique if applied at the critical moment an attacker turns in to you with, say, a hip technique. It is also a technique that is part of *nage-no-kata*, a very basic *kata* of throws which every *judoka* will be expected to perform at some time in order to progress their *judo* career. Exactly when that may be could depend upon whichever governing body they or their club are affiliated to.

There are some aspects of *ura-nage* which could become dangerous if not considered when practising the technique. To begin with, *tori* must throw himself to breakfall backwards when delivering the throw and must therefore keep his head well forward with his chin tucked in to avoid it whiplashing onto the mat. Some recommend that *tori* looks down towards the knot of his own belt when falling backwards.

At the other end, *uke* is subject to a very heavy fall from a properly executed *ura-nage* and for this reason at least it is not a throw to be performed against anyone less than fully experienced in breakfalling.

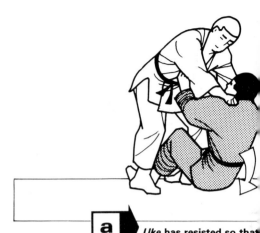

a *Uke* has resisted so that *tori* has lost backward momentum. Collapsing rather than throwing himself to the rear...

1 For a clearer view of what happens during the execution of this technique, *tori* is shown applying *ura-nage* to *uke*'s left side. Above is the critical moment at which *uke* is vulnerable to the counter throw as he turns out from his own attacking hip technique.

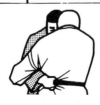

Rear view shows *tori* pulling *uke* in close with a strong right-hand grip on the back of *uke*'s belt.

2 *Tori* steps well forward. The heel of his left hand is moved to press hard against *uke*'s abdomen.

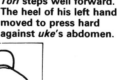

3 *Tori* drops to his rear, taking *uke* off balance forwards. He pulls with right hand on *uke*'s belt and pushes with his left his left arm is already beginning to extend in preparation for the major part of the throw over the top of *tori*.

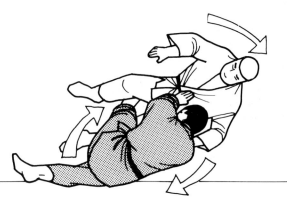

b ▶ ...but without losing all momentum, he immediately regains the initiative by hooking his left instep against *uke*'s inner upper right thigh...

c ▶ ...in order to co-ordinate a *sumi-gaeshi* leg action with a strong body twist and rotating arms. He completes the throw over his right shoulder.

4 ▶ *Tori*'s left arm is now fully extended to a final push while the right arm pulls as *uke* is turned across *tori*'s right shoulder towards his breakfall.

5 ▶ As *tori* pushes *uke* clear of his right shoulder, with the help of a final body twist, he lets go of *uke*'s belt with his right hand in order to execute his own breakfall.

View from the opposite side shows *tori*'s right hand pulling through on *uke*'s belt.

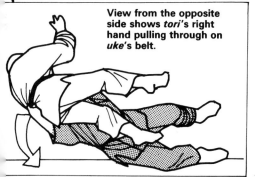

SUMI-GAESHI Corner throw

Sumi-gaeshi is an ideal technique for use against an opponent who adopts a crouching, defensive stance or simply drops into that posture because of fatigue. Then, he is drawn off balance to a front corner and is thrown, as the name of the technique implies, over that corner with *sumi-gaeshi*.

Practice will help the student synchronise the hooking action of the leg and foot with the drop backwards. He needs to co-ordinate both with a strong rotating arm action. In fact, the technique will just not work properly until all these movements have become blended into a fluid sequence. As with so many *judo* techniques, but especially sacrifice throws, he who hesitates is lost. There must be a full on-going commitment from beginning to end. Stop or falter mid-way and a player is lucky not to lose the initiative.

The hooking leg action from behind an opponent's thigh can be adapted to supplement other techniques in which *uke*'s resistance has brought a half-way halt to *tori*'s attack, and some of these instances are shown on other pages.

As recommended with all *judo* techniques practise *sumi-gaeshi* from both left and right sides, remembering that it's the foot opposite the shoulder over which the throw is to be made which is brought to hook beneath *uke*'s inner thigh.

1 As *uke* is beginning to crouch and lean forwards, *tori* has released his opponent's left lapel and has slipped his right hand to a preferred grip immediately to the rear of *uke*'s armpit. *Tori* lifts and pulls with his right hand while pulling forwards hard on *uke*'s right sleeve with his left hand. This forces *uke* to step forwards with his right foot in an attempt to retain his balance.

2 *Tori* steps his left leg deeply between *uke*'s feet and, still drawing *uke* to his front right corner, prepares to drop backwards.

3 As *tori* drops, or rolls, backwards, he simultaneously hooks his right instep against *uke*'s top inner left thigh, pushing and pulling to off balance *uke*.

Tori may reach over *uke*'s right shoulder to grab the belt before rolling sideways into a variation known popularly as 'the dustbin throw'.

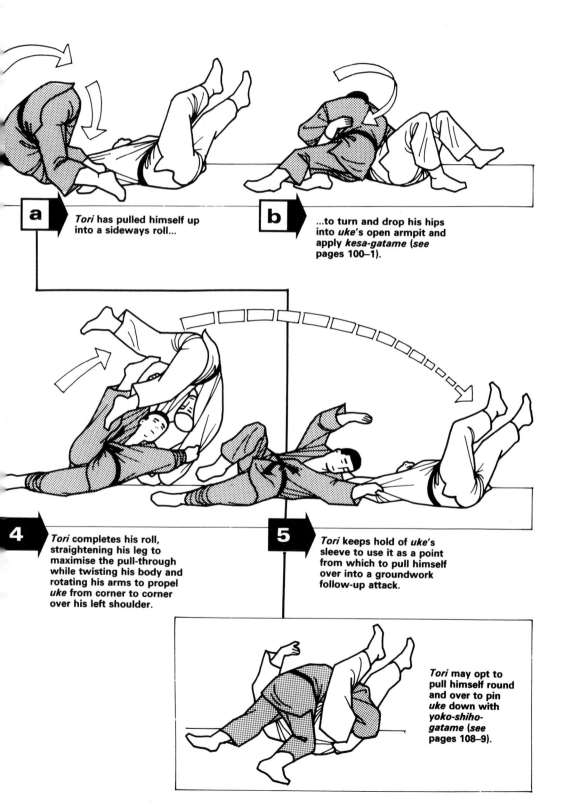

a ▶ *Tori* has pulled himself up into a sideways roll...

b ▶ ...to turn and drop his hips into *uke*'s open armpit and apply *kesa-gatame* (*see* pages 100–1).

4 ▶ *Tori* completes his roll, straightening his leg to maximise the pull-through while twisting his body and rotating his arms to propel *uke* from corner to corner over his left shoulder.

5 ▶ *Tori* keeps hold of *uke*'s sleeve to use it as a point from which to pull himself over into a groundwork follow-up attack.

Tori may opt to pull himself round and over to pin *uke* down with *yoko-shiho-gatame* (*see* pages 108–9).

YOKO-GAKE Side dash

Commonly referred to as 'side dash' or 'side body drop', the use of the word *gake* in the Japanese name would indicate that a hooking movement of some sort comes in somewhere during the execution of *yoko-gake*.

If it does, then it is in a subtle manner, as the sweeping action of *tori*'s attacking leg plants the inturned sole of the foot around the back of *uke*'s heel to hook or sweep it as *tori* and *uke* fall to their rears. The *gake* is not at all like the aggressively accentuated hooking movement in, for instance, the *kosoto-gake* shown on pages 72–3.

The initial movements of *yoko-gake* are very similar to those of *sasae-tsuri-komi-ashi* (see pages 60–1), but the sweep of the attacking leg is lower, with the outer edge of the curled-in foot skimming the mat. It makes contact with the outside of *uke*'s foot and is pushed right through as *tori* becomes committed to a sideway sacrifice throw.

Tori's left arm action is important in drawing *uke* forwards and yet off balance to his side. The action begins high to draw *uke* forwards and off

balance. It then whips outwards and downwards in a semi-circular arc to help twist *uke* further off balance to his rear right corner and in support of the foot sweep.

a It is not uncommon duri[ng] sacrifice technique attac[k] for *uke* to resist a less th[an] totally committed opponent and force *tori* into a collapsed sitting posture...

1 *Tori* wthdraws his left leg, opening his left side and thereby adding power to the high forward pull on his opponent's right sleeve. This forces *uke* to step forwards with his right foot in an attempt to regain balance to his front right corner.

2 With toes curled under, *tori* attacks *uke*'s heel with the sole of his left foot, simultaneously pulling outwards and downwards with his left hand.

3 *Tori*'s sole hooks behin[d] the back of *uke*'s heel t[o] begin the sweep as *tor[i]* drives off the right foot t[o] take *uke* with him as h[e] falls sideways.

This aerial view shows how, as *tori* falls with leg extended, his right arm is extended to push out far and wide. By contrast, his left arm is bent and pulled close with the hand towards his left hip. This contrasting arm action helps to turn *uke* and propel him onto his back. Also, the tucked-in left elbow saves it from possible injury as *tori* falls to the mat.

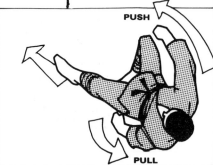

PUSH

PULL

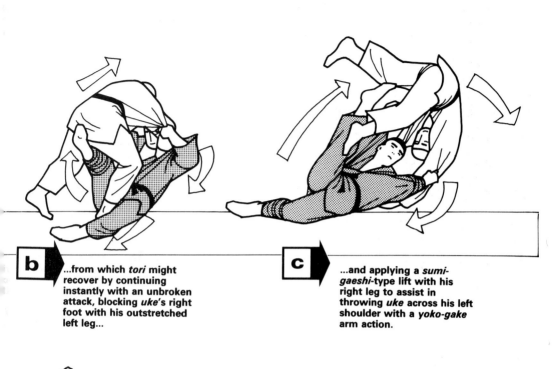

b ...from which *tori* might recover by continuing instantly with an unbroken attack, blocking *uke*'s right foot with his outstretched left leg...

c ...and applying a *sumi-gaeshi*-type lift with his right leg to assist in throwing *uke* across his left shoulder with a *yoko-gake* arm action.

4 *Tori* extends his sweep as he breakfalls to the mat first, retaining hold of *uke*'s right sleeve and using it immediately as a point from which to pull himself close to *uke* and into groundwork. *Tori*'s co-ordinated use of leg sweep, arm action and falling bodyweight take *uke* into the air, his push-and-pull arm action having turned *uke* in flight so that he falls back first towards the mat.

5 As *uke* breakfalls, *tori* pulls on the retained right sleeve to turn himself into a position from which there will be easy access to groundwork.

This shows how *tori* was quite easily able to pull himself through into *yoko-shiho-gatame* (see pages 108–9).

YOKO-OTOSHI Side drop

Yoko-otoshi depends very much for success upon you being able to recruit your opponent's own weight and energy force in order to bring about what is a powerful throw.

Assuming that the *yoko-otoshi* is to be applied to your opponent's right side, then your opponent must be moving towards his right side at the time of launching the attack. The critical moment the attack must begin is in the course of transferring his weight from his left foot to his right; in fact, when he is just about to place the weight upon his right foot. *That* is the critical moment for *tori* to drop into attack.

Failing that, *tori* must feint to *uke*'s left side and then, as *uke*'s reflex action prompts him to pull back towards the right, *tori* must go in that direction also, adding his energy to that of *uke*'s and thereby multiplying the force which will be put into the throw to *uke*'s right side.

Like all *sutemi-waza* attacks, *yoko-otoshi* demands of *tori* full commitment, confidence and no doubt of the ability to follow through if necessary with a proficient standard of groundwork.

a Again, *tori*'s attacking *sutemi-waza* breaks down and he collapses to a sitting posture, but with hesitation...

1 *Tori* and *uke* are facing each other in normal right-hand postures as *tori* feints to force *uke* to his right side.

2 *Uke* resists and, as he transfers his weight back towards his right, *tori* goes with him and extends his left foot forwards.

3 *Tori* drops to his left side extending his left leg to outside of *uke*'s right foot and pulling *uke* off balance to his front right corner.

This aerial view of the contestants shows what some may regard as a better grip of *uke*'s jacket as *tori* prefers to get more purchase out of the right arm action by taking a right-hand grip of the jacket at *uke*'s front armpit.

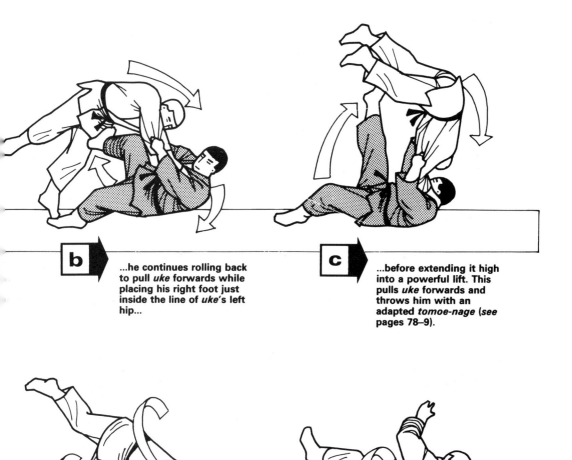

b ...he continues rolling back to pull *uke* forwards while placing his right foot just inside the line of *uke*'s left hip...

c ...before extending it high into a powerful lift. This pulls *uke* forwards and throws him with an adapted *tomoe-nage* (*see* pages 78–9).

4 *Tori*'s left leg has skimmed over the mat to full extension, brushing the inside calf against the outside of *uke*'s right ankle. Combined with *tori*'s fully committed body drop, and rotating arm action, this pulls *uke* well forwards and he is tipped off balance over *tori*'s outstretched leg.

5 As his opponent falls to his front right corner, *tori* shortens his left arm in order to help turn *uke* over.

Tori's shortened left arm has pulled *uke* close in on landing and is conveniently placed for *tori* to roll over into groundwork.

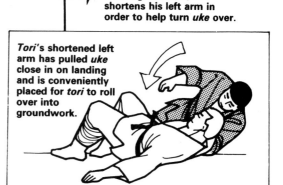

TANI-O-TOSHI Valley drop

With such a dramatic translation of its name as 'valley drop', it would be fair to expect a technique much grander in execution than *tani-o-toshi* appears to be. It is, however, effective and probably derives its name from the manner in which *tori* draws *uke* through the 'valley' of his widely spreadeagled legs.

Tani-otoshi is in fact a deeper form of *yoko-otoshi* (*see* pages 86–7), requiring *tori* to step into an opponent much further, establishing strong forward body contact and sweeping the attacking leg as far as possible around the back of *uke*'s legs.

An important element of the attack, if being made to *uke*'s right side, is that it helps unbalance *uke* to his rear right corner by pulling his right sleeve straight down towards the back of his own feet – not out sideways or to the rear, but straight down and synchronised with the unbalancing leg sweep in the opposite direction.

The toes of *tori*'s attacking foot should be pointed and then curled under as the outside edge of the foot skims across the mat.

a As *uke* is able to resist t attack by attempting an *uchi-gari* counter to *tor* rear, *tori* retreats, taking the advancing energy fo with him as he drops to rear.

1 At close quarters, *tori* feints to his opponent's left and then, as *uke* resists and automatically pulls back, *tori* rocks with him towards the original right side.

2 As energy forces are joined towards *uke*'s right, *tori* slips his right hand through *uke*'s left armpit to grasp the jacket at the rear in order to apply forearm lifting leverage towards *uke*'s right. Simultaneously, *tori*'s left hand pulls down on *uke*'s right sleeve as *tori* leans his body forwards to sweep his left leg forwards, and to close in around the back of *uke*'s right leg.

3 *Tori* establishes strong upper body contact wi *uke*, driving off the bac foot and sweeping fur around *uke*'s legs with left leg.
There's a continuing upward leverage towa *uke*'s right from *tori*'s forearm beneath the a and a straight down pe *uke*'s right sleeve.

b He simultaneously raises his right leg to curl the instep against the inside top of *uke*'s left thigh...

c ...then extends it as for *sumi-gaeshi* (yes, again!) and throws him across his left shoulder.

4 As *tori*'s sweeping leg is pushed across the back of *uke*'s legs, his bodyweight passes across his opponent's point of balance and *uke* begins to fall to his rear.

5 *Tori* swivels to his left off his right foot as he drops backwards.

6 *Uke* is spiralled clear over *tori*'s extended leg.

YOKO-WAKARE Side separation

Yoko-wakare can be one of the most spectacular of all sacrifice techniques. At first, it seems to be a throw for *judo*'s dedicated strong men who have the utmost confidence in themselves and who also possess the strength of arm necessary to propel an opponent, without body contact, into a throw which carries him through the air from one side to the other of their supine, spread-eagled body.

Having said that, confidence and commitment are not the sole prerogative of strong men. Also, the degree of muscle power required is variable, depending as it does for most throws upon the purist *judo* principle of choosing the right critical moment at which your opponent's advancing bodyweight may become merged with that of your own power to provide a multiplied energy force which can be harnessed and used for your own requirements.

a   **Uke** has resisted **tori**'s attack, pulling back to rear...

1   **Tori** feints to his opponent's left and, as **uke** resists and pulls to his right, **tori** instantly switches his attack back to that direction also.

2   **Tori**'s withdrawal of the left foot and opening up of his left side add power to the high sleeve pull.

3   **Tori** extends his right le[g] down the outside of uk[e's] right. He drops backwa[rd]

As with *yoko-otoshi* (*see* pages 86–7) **tori** takes a right-hand grip of **uke**'s jacket at the front of his left armpit.

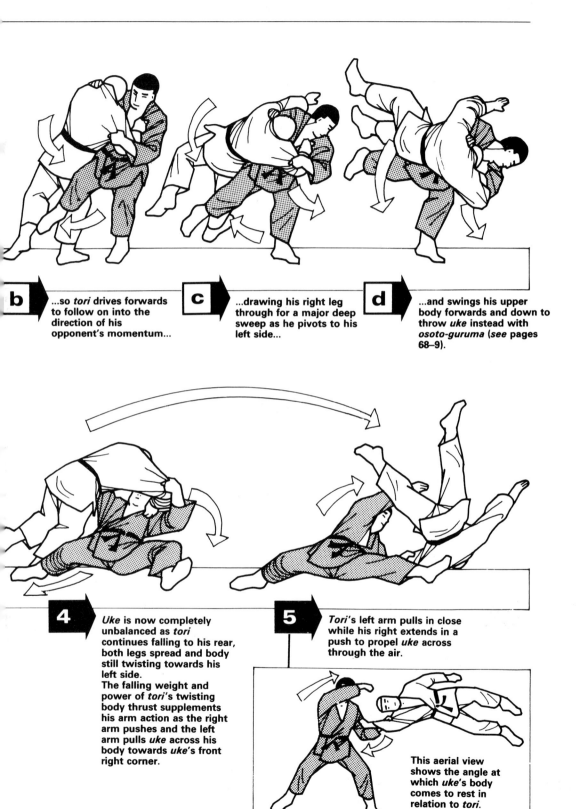

b ...so *tori* drives forwards to follow on into the direction of his opponent's momentum...

c ...drawing his right leg through for a major deep sweep as he pivots to his left side...

d ...and swings his upper body forwards and down to throw *uke* instead with *osoto-guruma* (*see* pages 68–9).

4 *Uke* is now completely unbalanced as *tori* continues falling to his rear, both legs spread and body still twisting towards his left side.
The falling weight and power of *tori*'s twisting body thrust supplements his arm action as the right arm pushes and the left arm pulls *uke* across his body towards *uke*'s front right corner.

5 *Tori*'s left arm pulls in close while his right extends in a push to propel *uke* across through the air.

This aerial view shows the angle at which *uke*'s body comes to rest in relation to *tori*.

UKI-WAZA Floating throw

Uki-waza is historically one of *judo*'s classical techniques and, though seldom used in present-day contests, it is included in *nage-no-kata*, a basic *kata* which every *judoka* will have to perform at some stage of their *judo* career, depending upon the syllabus of their club's parent association.

The basic principles, qualities demanded and method of executing *uki-waza* are in some ways similar to those of *yoko-otoshi* (*see* pages 86–7). One outstanding difference is that in *uki-waza*, shown here, there is no sliding leg contact with the outer side of *uke*'s legs. As with *yoko-wakare* (*see* pages 90–1), *uke* is carried solely by the combined power of body twist and rotating arm action across *tori*'s shoulder without any leg or body contact. *Uke* is wheeled across *tori*'s shoulder in much the same way as in *yoko-wakare*, excepting of course that in *uki-waza* the leading foot of *uke* is positioned on the mat at some point *between* the outstretched legs of *tori* and not to the *outside* of both of *tori*'s legs.

Although an apparently simple technique, like other sacrifice throws it depends for success upon critical timing and the exploitation of your opponent's own advancing weight and forward energy forces.

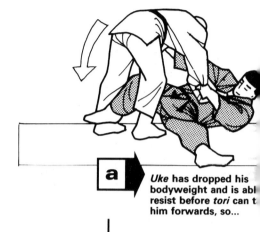

a Uke has dropped his bodyweight and is abl resist before *tori* can t him forwards, so...

1 Tori and *uke* are facing each other in normal right-hand postures as *tori* feints to his opponent's left. Then, as *uke* pulls back towards his right side, *tori* reverts and pushes in that direction also.

2 At the critical moment *uke* is transferring his bodyweight back onto his right foot, *tori* drops straight backwards, pulling on *uke*'s front jacket with his right hand and on his right sleeve with his left. Simultaneously, *tori* slides his left leg straight forwards over the mat, clear to the outside of his opponent's right foot, at which time *uke*'s own advancing weight helps to ensure he's taken well off balance to his front right corner.

3 Tori is able to drive off right foot, adding powe that of his body twist i support of the strong revolving arm action w is now beginning to tip forwards over his front right corner. Tori is alre pushing upwards and o with his right arm whil shortening his left arm order to turn *uke* onto back as he floats across *tori*'s left shoulder.

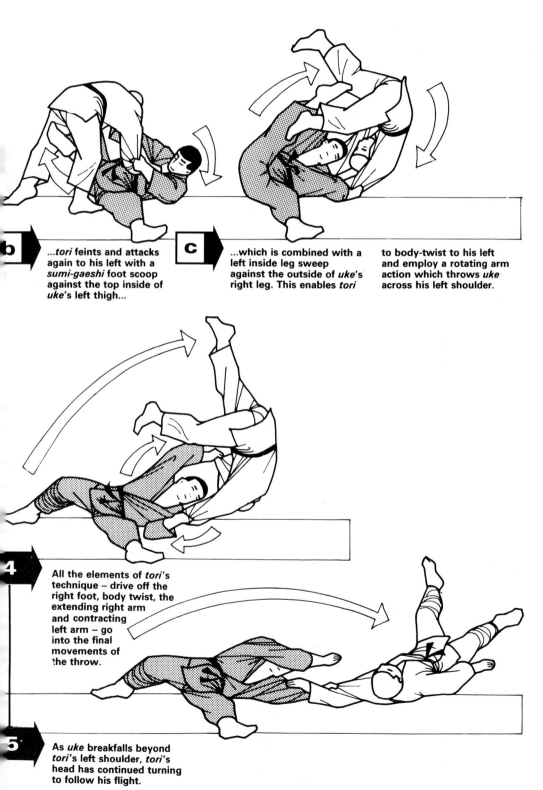

b ...*tori* feints and attacks again to his left with a *sumi-gaeshi* foot scoop against the top inside of *uke*'s left thigh...

c ...which is combined with a left inside leg sweep against the outside of *uke*'s right leg. This enables *tori* to body-twist to his left and employ a rotating arm action which throws *uke* across his left shoulder.

4 All the elements of *tori*'s technique – drive off the right foot, body twist, the extending right arm and contracting left arm – go into the final movements of the throw.

5 As *uke* breakfalls beyond *tori*'s left shoulder, *tori*'s head has continued turning to follow his flight.

YOKO-GURUMA Side wheel

Rather than being a single direct attack in its own right, *yoko-guruma* is predominantly a very useful counter which may be applied to good effect against any of a wide range of popular attacking throws. It is particularly useful against an opponent who 'offers' a leading leg, or allows you the opportunity of stepping around him as he turns in to attack.

Yoko-guruma requires all the positive thinking, instant reaction and critical commitment to follow-through as do any of the so-called sacrifice techniques. However, remember that as a *yoko* form of *sutemi-waza*, the commitment of *tori* is not to fall directly backwards, but to execute more of an outstretched sliding roll onto his side.

The step-around, the sliding leg, body-twisting fall to the side back corner and the revolving arms being carried up beyond the head must all be combined into one composite action. Practising the combined movement repeatedly, without a partner, will help to inspire a *judoka*'s confidence in throwing himself freely, without inhibition, into the *yoko-guruma* technique.

a At this point, *uke* may ▮ quick enough to pull ba▮ to his right in resistanc▮ *tori* counters by feintin▮ and attacking again to *uke*'s right side...

1 As *uke* turns in to attack with *tai-o-toshi*, *tori* blocks by dropping his hips.

2 *Tori* instantly pivots to take his right leg over *uke*'s right.

3 *Tori* continues his turn▮ face *uke*'s front, taking▮ left-hand grip at the ba▮ *uke*'s belt as his right ▮ slides deeply between ▮ *uke*'s feet.
Tori has by now accumulated a right-to▮ turning momentum w▮ must be maintained throughout the techni▮

Reverse view shows the step-around *tori* will have to make in order to swing into a *yoko-guruma* counter against *uke*'s attacking *tai-o-toshi*.

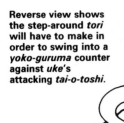

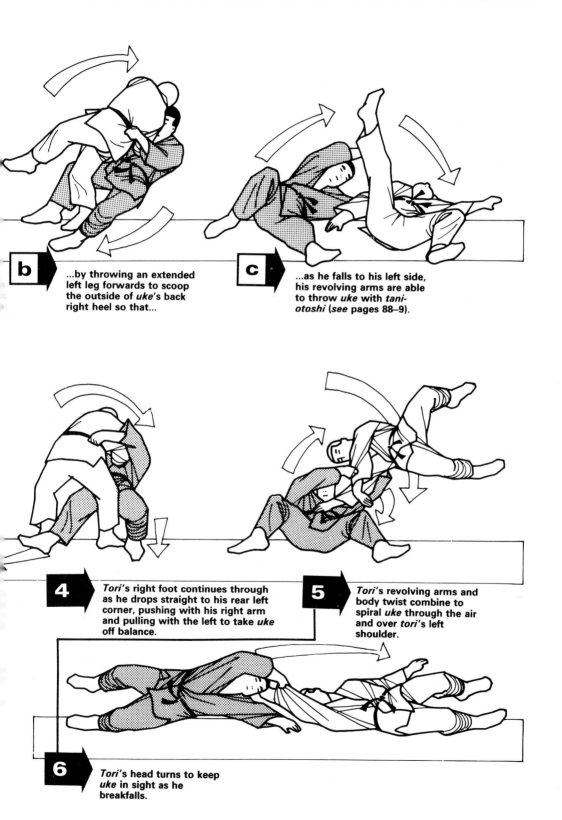

b ...by throwing an extended left leg forwards to scoop the outside of *uke*'s back right heel so that...

c ...as he falls to his left side, his revolving arms are able to throw *uke* with *tani-otoshi* (*see* pages 88–9).

4 *Tori*'s right foot continues through as he drops straight to his rear left corner, pushing with his right arm and pulling with the left to take *uke* off balance.

5 *Tori*'s revolving arms and body twist combine to spiral *uke* through the air and over *tori*'s left shoulder.

6 *Tori*'s head turns to keep *uke* in sight as he breakfalls.

SOTO-MAKIKOMI Outer wrap-around throw

If not always the basic *soto-makikomi*, then a *makikomi* variation of some sort must be in the repertoire of any contest *judoka*. Delivered properly, so as to achieve maximum impact, any *makikomi* can be a devastating throw and a real match winner. The fall from a *makikomi* is usually heavy and it's therefore not a technique to be recommended to beginners, at least not until they've become hardened and fully experienced at breakfalling.

It cannot be said too often that sacrifice throws demand one hundred per cent commitment on the part of *tori*. It might be added that a *makikomi* demands even more. *Tori* must generate sufficient circular propulsion to spin both his opponent and himself off their feet with such power, as he literally wraps *uke* around him in mid-air, that the pair of them become locked together and remain so until they crash onto the mat.

The raised, circling action of *tori*'s enveloping arm is a distinctive recognition of a *makikomi* being performed, whether it be the basic *makikomi* shown here or any of the variations referred to.

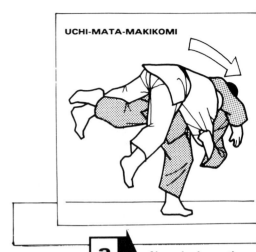

UCHI-MATA-MAKIKOMI

a Above is shown the distinctive wrap-around arm action of *soto-makikomi* combining w the inner thigh leg swe of *uchi-mata* (*see* page 66–7) as *tori* executes mata-makikomi.

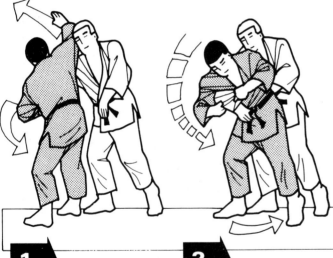

1 As *tori* pulls on *uke*'s sleeve, he turns to raise his right arm.

Reverse view showing how deliberately *tori* pulls *uke*'s upper forearm through his armpit.

2 *Tori* pivots to swing his left leg around to his rear so that his back is turned towards *uke*. He is still pulling on *uke*'s right arm so that it becomes wrapped closely in to his own front body.
At the same time, *tori* leans forwards with his armpit over *uke*'s right arm, swinging his own right arm in a continuing curve over the top.

3 In a non-stop revolvin motion, *tori* continues turning to his left, preparing to drive int momentum off his left *Uke*'s right arm contir to be pulled through right armpit while tor own right arm comple its swing to clamp the captured arm even m *Uke* is now moving completely off balanc his front right corner.

HARAI-MAKIKOMI

HANE-MAKIKOMI

b ▶ Here is the *makikomi* arm and rotating body in combination with a *harai-goshi* sweeping loin (*see* pages 28–9) as *tori* executes *harai-makikomi*.

c ▶ The distinctive arm and rotating body action can also be combined with the spring-hip action of *hane-goshi* (*see* pages 20–1) as *tori* executes what is called *hane-makikomi*.

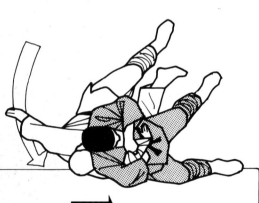

4 ▶ *Tori* is fully committed, having continued to hurl himself and *uke* into circular rotation in an anti-clockwise direction, the combined bodyweight of both contributing to the force of the throw.

5 ▶ The actual breakfall is usually heavy, *tori* keeping his own right elbow tucked in safe from injury.

From this position, *tori* may retain his right arm grip of *uke*'s arm and roll to his left up into a variation of *ushiro-kesa-gatame* (*see* pages 102–3).

ABOUT KATA

Kata means 'form' and in *judo* it refers to what might be described as a choreographed set of prearranged movements and techniques performed in sequence by *tori* with a co-operative *uke*. There is more than one *kata*. Each *kata* is comprised of a number of prearranged movements related by a single theme and performed by *tori* and *uke* in harmony with each other.

The three most common *kata* in the western world are called *Nage-no-kata* (Throwing Forms), *Katame-no-kata* (Grappling Forms) and *Ju-no-kata* (The Form of Gentleness).

All the individual techniques included in *Nage-no-kata* and *Katame-no-kata* are featured in this book. Not all are included in general syllabus work, although this varies throughout *judo* from one parent body to another.

Practically none of the techniques contained within *Ju-no-kata* are within any syllabus work and because they are outside the sport of *judo* they are not demonstrated in this book. Despite its 'gentle' name, *Ju-no-kata* is comprised very much of a series of self-defence techniques linked together in sequence.

Knowing how to perform the individual techniques contained in any *kata* is simple and straightforward. The challenge is in perfecting the manner of their performance in relation to each other. The techniques within a *kata* have to be performed in a certain way, in a certain specified sequence at a smooth but moderate speed, and they have to be linked by particular patterns of footwork moving the actions in certain directions.

Techniques are performed to both left and right sides, with *tori* and *uke* working in harmony, exchanging respects at fixed intervals with themselves and the adjudicators.

The adjudicators assessing *tori*'s performance will be senior *dan* grades experienced in the teaching and performance of *kata*.

Exactly how to link together the movements of any *kata* is a more complex matter than can be dealt with as part of a book such as this and in any case there are variances between different authorities outside the Kodokan on some particular aspects of style and interpretation. It is a subject to discuss with your own *sensei* who, if not sufficiently experienced in the subject himself, may be able to provide a calendar of *kata* courses for interested students in your district.

Whether or not a *judoka* moves into the study of *kata* may depend upon the qualifying requirements of a club's parent body, apart from any personal choice. The British Judo Council, for instance, requires all affiliated members to display progressing degrees of ability in *Nage-no-kata* and *Katame-no-kata* during grading examinations from Green Belt (3rd *Kyu*) upwards. Additionally, female members are tested in the performance of *Ju-no-kata* rather than solely upon their contest ability and syllabus work.

The whole idea of grouping sets of related techniques within a *kata* was part of Professor Jigoro Kano's original concept of how *judo* should be taught and learned. His early instructors had to demonstrate *kata* proficiency before being allowed to teach.

There are many today who believe the whole idea of *kata* has become outdated and unnecessary, it having been pushed into the background by the popularity of competitive *judo*. On the other hand, traditional purists believe that it is only through *kata* that a student will discover the true essence of what *judo* is all about: the marriage of physical and mental abilities.

It cannot be denied that ignorance of *kata* in favour of a syllabus-based learning process mixed with *randori* does enable a student to enjoy competitive *judo* after having gained very little experience or depth of knowledge. The student often discovers that good enough results can be achieved on the basis of having mastered only a very confined range of 'favourite' techniques.

After such competitive excitement, the chore of virtually going back to the technical drawing board of *judo kata* with its learning processes and slowed-down action seems to many a very dull prospect and they never widen their scope of either technical or spiritual knowledge.

Beyond the three forms of *kata* referred to others included are called *Kime-no-kata* (Forms of Decision), *Goshin-jutsu* (Self-defence Forms), *Itsutsu-no-kata* (The Five Forms) and *Koshiki-no-kata* (Ancient Forms).

Apart from the knowledge gained and improvement of technical ability through the study of *kata*, there is also the competitive element: *kata* tournament entrants compete against each other for points awarded for such things as technical ability, style interpretation and general presentation.

oundwork might seem at first to present the ginner with a completely new set of skills to be quired. Yet, upon closer examination, it will be en that the same basic principles of *judo* apply much to *katame-waza* as they do to *nage-waza*. uch of an attacker's success on the ground (or at!) is dependent at some stage upon taking an ponent off balance or transposing his energy or vancing bodyweight into a force which can be ed against him.

During the execution of throwing techniques, e 'corners' which surround a *judoka* are gener-y invisible points of direction over which an ponent may be manoeuvered in order to disturb lance. Sometimes, they are drawn off balance to e front over a lowered centre of gravity, which is other invisible marking.

However, during groundwork, most of the in-ible 'corners' to a defender's points of balance e often very visible indeed and should therefore much easier to exploit.

The simplest example is to imagine yourself d your opponent facing one another in an right kneeling posture, each taking a normal p of each other's right sleeve and left lapel. ur knees now represent feet as if you were in a nding posture. To extend one of your legs wards and use the curled-in sole of the foot to sh one of your opponent's knees backwards as u pull forwards to the same side would collapse e side of his kneeling posture and draw him off lance to the front corner.

Next, imagine your opponent to be crouched ward on hands (or, more likely, elbows) and es in a typical defensive posture. He has four ible corners which are vulnerable to attack in ler to disturb his points of balance. There are hands, or elbows, at the front end and two es at the other. Remove any one of them by ling, pushing or scooping and your opponent collapse to that corner.

hat is the principle, or theory! There are in-merable ways in which a *judoka* sets about ieving this in practice as players grapple to noeuvre an opponent into one of the *katame-za* techniques set out in the following pages.

n the course of grappling, the use of bodyweight nother important contribution to success. To a ser sensational degree perhaps than in *nage-za*, it is possible to exploit an opponent's lyweight and energy forces by reversing pulls oushes against limbs and the body itself.

What is of special importance during ground-rk, especially during hold-downs or pinning nniques, is proper control of your own body-ght distribution. Try bringing your full body-ght to bear down on your opponent at all es. The skill of moving around an opponent at ed while still retaining full bodyweight press-can be practised in a simple exercise with a tner.

Your partner lies down, face upwards. As domi-nator, you lie across him at right angles, crossing at about the solar plexus point, with your face facing downwards. Hold your arms out above your head, with your legs spreadeagled behind you and the toes of your feet turned under.

Then, swinging your arms in a clockwise direc-tion at the front and pushing off from your toes at the back end, your body can revolve in a flat, spin-ning movement centred on the abdomen. Circular momentum is accumulated and maintained by pushing off alternate feet as you revolve.

Your partner's arms remain still by his sides. Your own arms never grasp your partner but are swung loose to help maintain the spinning momentum. Reverse the spin frequently to revolve in the opposite direction. A similar spinning exercise may be performed as you lay face down to spin around across your opponent's back while he crouches face down to the mat in a curled-up defensive posture.

During groundwork, the maintenance of maxi-mum body contact prevents gaps occurring against which an opponent may be able to bridge or twist, or through which he may be able to push an arm or leg and be on the way to escaping or counter-ing the effect of whatever technique you may be applying at the time.

The whole area of *katame-waza* is divided into three categories of techniques. They are:

- *Osae-komi-waza* which comprises hold-down or pinning techniques
- *Kansetsu-waza* which comprises only arm-lock techniques
- *Shime-waza* which comprises strangle tech-niques.

Needless to say, all *katame-waza* should be prac-tised from both left and right sides. In the follow-ing pages, whichever side shows best just what is going on has been chosen for demonstration.

KESA-GATAME Scarf hold

The basic or *hon-kesa-gatame* is very often the first hold-down technique taught to beginners. This is probably because it provides such a good practical example of what is repeatedly advised: if you retain hold of an opponent's arm during a throw and into the breakfall, it will make way for an instant follow-through into groundwork.

The upward stretch on an opponent's retained arm opens up the armpit to provide a perfect cockpit into which *tori* can drop his hips while moving from standing posture into this particular groundwork technique.

Although predominantly regarded as a hold-down technique, *kesa-gatame* can sometimes result in *uke* tapping in submission if it is executed so that *tori*'s weight is applied in a particular manner. A *judoka* will sometimes have his hips so far down the side of *uke*'s body, away from the armpit, that he's almost laying by the side of his opponent. This is totally wrong and ineffective.

The effective method is to sit into the armpit, bending forwards, but leaning sideways so your bodyweight presses into *uke*'s lower rib cage. This is the part which can well become unbearable and bring about the submission.

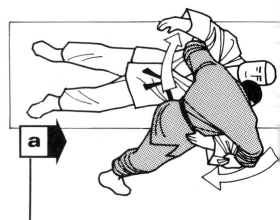

a

At this point, *tori* may choose instead to pass his left arm to the underside of *uke*'s right arm, sliding his flat hand, palm down, forwards over the mat...

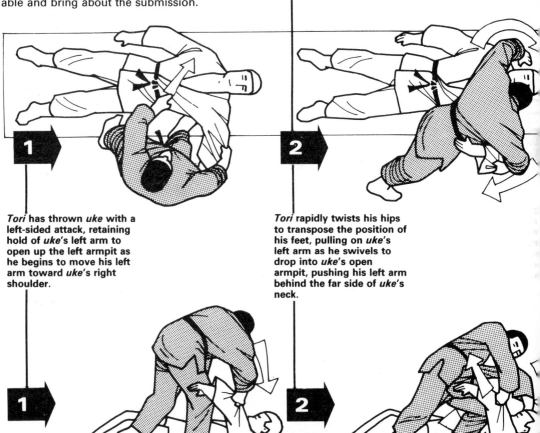

1

Tori has thrown *uke* with a left-sided attack, retaining hold of *uke*'s left arm to open up the left armpit as he begins to move his left arm toward *uke*'s right shoulder.

2

Tori rapidly twists his hips to transpose the position of his feet, pulling on *uke*'s left arm as he swivels to drop into *uke*'s open armpit, pushing his left arm behind the far side of *uke*'s neck.

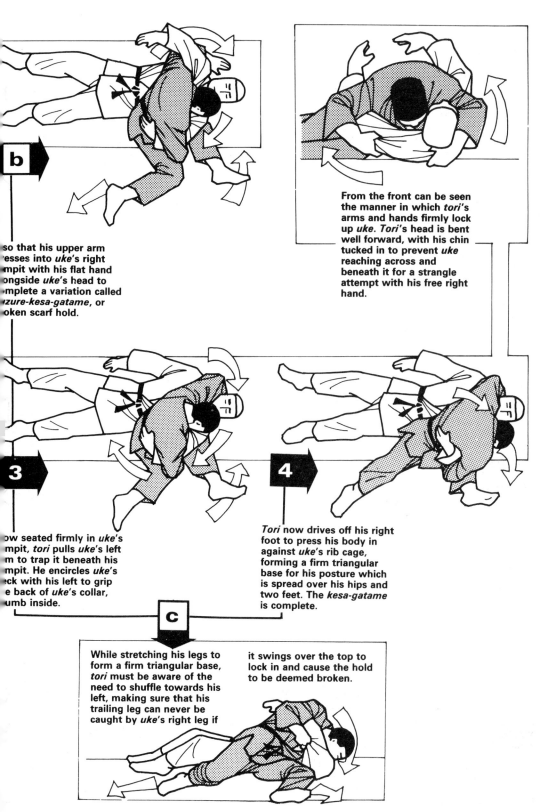

b

so that his upper arm
esses into *uke*'s right
mpit with his flat hand
ongside *uke*'s head to
mplete a variation called
zure-kesa-gatame, or
oken scarf hold.

From the front can be seen
the manner in which *tori*'s
arms and hands firmly lock
up *uke*. *Tori*'s head is bent
well forward, with his chin
tucked in to prevent *uke*
reaching across and
beneath it for a strangle
attempt with his free right
hand.

3

ow seated firmly in *uke*'s
mpit, *tori* pulls *uke*'s left
m to trap it beneath his
mpit. He encircles *uke*'s
ck with his left to grip
e back of *uke*'s collar,
umb inside.

4

Tori now drives off his right
foot to press his body in
against *uke*'s rib cage,
forming a firm triangular
base for his posture which
is spread over his hips and
two feet. The *kesa-gatame*
is complete.

c

While stretching his legs to
form a firm triangular base,
tori must be aware of the
need to shuffle towards his
left, making sure that his
trailing leg can never be
caught by *uke*'s right leg if

it swings over the top to
lock in and cause the hold
to be deemed broken.

USHIRO-KESA-GATAME Reverse scarf hold

It is sometimes possible to swivel on your bottom and transpose the position of your legs in order to move from the basic *hon-kesa-gatame* (*see* pages 100–1) into this *ushiro-kesa-gatame* variation of the scarf hold.

Otherwise, it can be dropped into immediately upon following through into groundwork after a throw, or a *judoka* may suddenly find himself able to apply it as an opportunist technique in the course of generally grappling for supremacy on the ground.

In *ushiro-kesa-gatame*, *tori* leans more across the top front of his opponent's rib cage, again pressing his head down and making sure his chin is tucked in to prevent *uke*'s free right arm from groping across the top in search of a countering strangle.

Also, it's advisable to lean well forwards so that you don't lay across *uke*'s face or in any way impede breathing through the nose and mouth. As with *hon-kesa-gatame*, the spreadeagled legs of *tori* contribute towards a strong, triangularly based form.

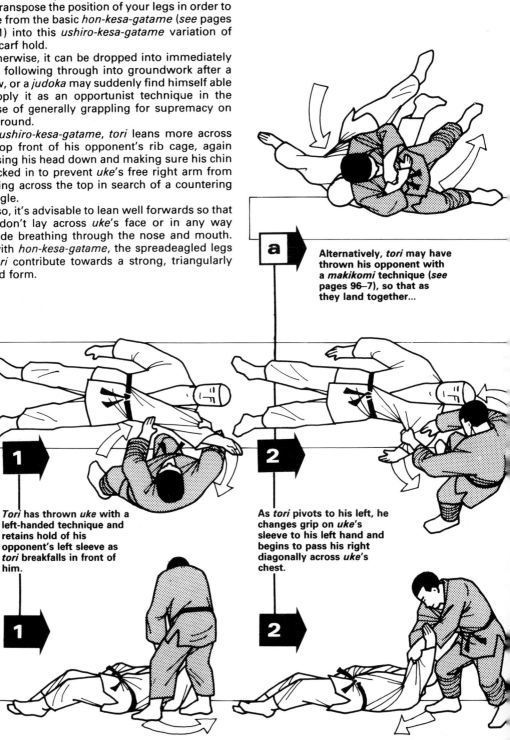

a Alternatively, *tori* may have thrown his opponent with a *makikomi* technique (*see* pages 96–7), so that as they land together...

1 *Tori* has thrown *uke* with a left-handed technique and retains hold of his opponent's left sleeve as *tori* breakfalls in front of him.

2 As *tori* pivots to his left, he changes grip on *uke*'s sleeve to his left hand and begins to pass his right diagonally across *uke*'s chest.

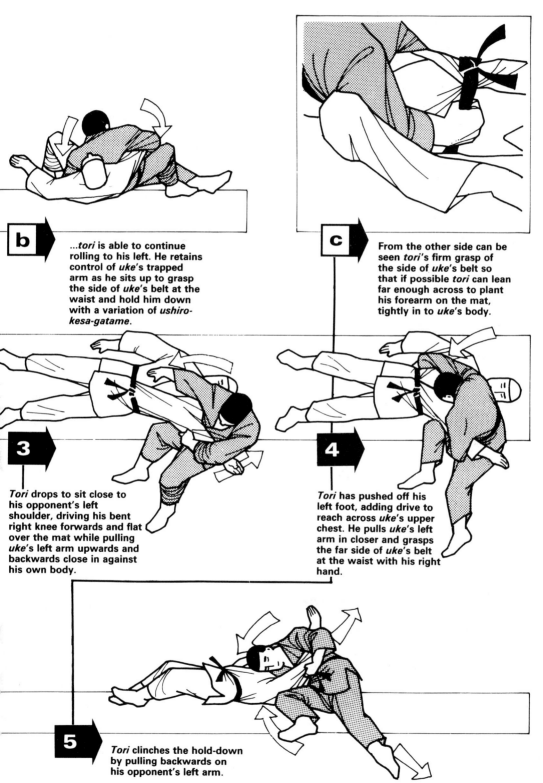

b ...*tori* is able to continue rolling to his left. He retains control of *uke*'s trapped arm as he sits up to grasp the side of *uke*'s belt at the waist and hold him down with a variation of *ushiro-kesa-gatame*.

c From the other side can be seen *tori*'s firm grasp of the side of *uke*'s belt so that if possible *tori* can lean far enough across to plant his forearm on the mat, tightly in to *uke*'s body.

3 *Tori* drops to sit close to his opponent's left shoulder, driving his bent right knee forwards and flat over the mat while pulling *uke*'s left arm upwards and backwards close in against his own body.

4 *Tori* has pushed off his left foot, adding drive to reach across *uke*'s upper chest. He pulls *uke*'s left arm in closer and grasps the far side of *uke*'s belt at the waist with his right hand.

5 *Tori* clinches the hold-down by pulling backwards on his opponent's left arm.

KATA-GATAME Shoulder hold

Kata-gatame is very often an attacking *judoka*'s follow-on to a *kesa-gatame* hold-down attempt from which *uke* manages to escape by freeing his trapped arm (*see* pages 100–1).

In such a case, *tori* will encourage *uke*'s freed arm to move across the front of his face, keeping it clear of his own throat by pushing behind the elbow. This will take the arm towards *uke*'s opposite side. Then as *tori* leans forwards to encircle *uke*'s head and one shoulder with his own arms he will press the side of his head against the outer side of *uke*'s arm to make it securely trapped.

As with *osae-komi* techniques, the use of *tori*'s legs are important in the application of *kata*-gatame. *Tori* drives off the foot of his outstretched leg and down through his raised hips to help bear bodyweight down upon *uke*. This supplements the power of his arm grip. The bent knee of *tori*'s other leg is on the mat, with the outside of the thigh wedged close into the side of *uke*'s upper body and restricting any body-twist attempt to escape.

The correct application of *kata-gatame* can bring about a submission from the strangulating effect of *tori*'s encircling arm against the side of *uke*'s neck.

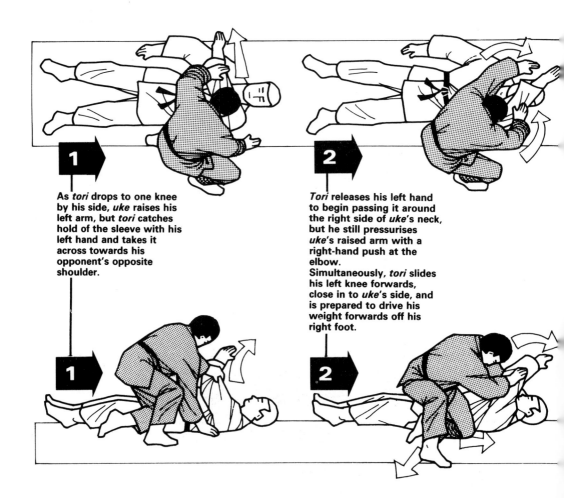

1 As *tori* drops to one knee by his side, *uke* raises his left arm, but *tori* catches hold of the sleeve with his left hand and takes it across towards his opponent's opposite shoulder.

2 *Tori* releases his left hand to begin passing it around the right side of *uke*'s neck, but he still pressurises *uke*'s raised arm with a right-hand push at the elbow.
Simultaneously, *tori* slides his left knee forwards, close in to *uke*'s side, and is prepared to drive his weight forwards off his right foot.

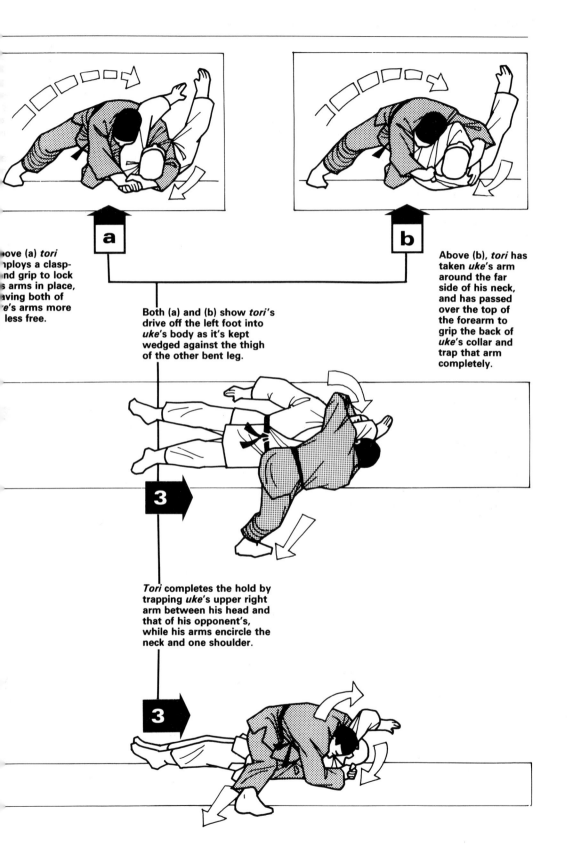

a

b

ove (a) *tori* ploys a clasp- nd grip to lock s arms in place, aving both of e's arms more less free.

Both (a) and (b) show *tori*'s drive off the left foot into *uke*'s body as it's kept wedged against the thigh of the other bent leg.

Above (b), *tori* has taken *uke*'s arm around the far side of his neck, and has passed over the top of the forearm to grip the back of *uke*'s collar and trap that arm completely.

3

Tori completes the hold by trapping *uke*'s upper right arm between his head and that of his opponent's, while his arms encircle the neck and one shoulder.

3

KAMI-SHIHO-GATAME Upper four quarter hold

Very often, the opportunity to apply *kami-shiho-gatame* comes about in the course of grappling generally for advantage. During such groundwork exchanges, *tori* may find it possible to roll into a position from which to apply *kami-shiho-gatame*.

Again comparing *nage-waza* (throwing techniques) with *katame-waza* (groundwork techniques) it can be seen that in *kami-shiho-gatame*, *tori* flattens down to spread his bodyweight over the support of his four 'corners' of balance. Two elbows at the front are tucked well into *uke*'s sides, but they rest on the mat and help to control

any attempt *uke* may make to rock or roll from side to side in a bid for escape. The in-turned toes of *tori*'s two feet provide 'corners' at his other end, unless his knees provide the same stability there is a need to draw one or even both up into the crouched position.

The movement of *tori*'s legs from outstretched to kneeling, either singly or together, plays major part in *tori*'s control of *uke*'s body movements. Pressure of *tori*'s head down onto *uke*'s abdomen helps prevent *uke* from attempting to bridge and twist his body into an escape attempt

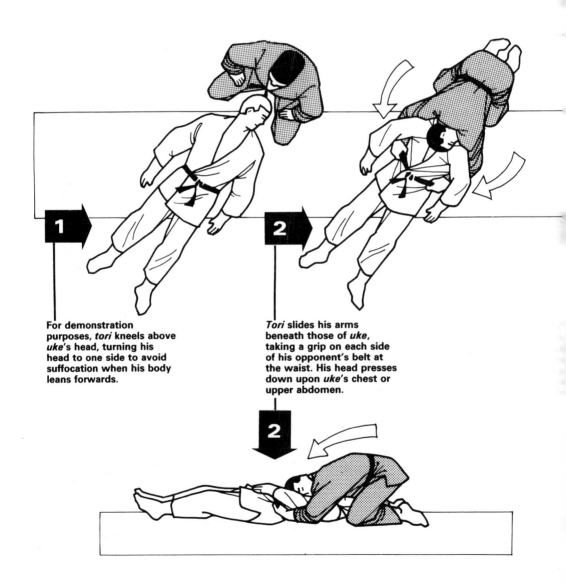

1 For demonstration purposes, *tori* kneels above *uke*'s head, turning his head to one side to avoid suffocation when his body leans forwards.

2 *Tori* slides his arms beneath those of *uke*, taking a grip on each side of his opponent's belt at the waist. His head presses down upon *uke*'s chest or upper abdomen.

b This shows the direction of *uke*'s hold-down power which is driven off the toes and down through his flattened hips to main body contact. His head pushes into *uke*'s upper abdomen while the arms are drawn in tightly.

a The top drawing shows the foot of the outstretched leg with the toes turned under. Below is shown the flattened instep from which comes only mat burns to toes and instep.

3 *Tori* draws his elbows in close to *uke*'s body, tightening the grip as the hold comes on and spreadeagling his legs to help control the movement of his opponent's body.

4 Depending upon the direction towards which *uke* struggles, *tori* may leave both legs extended, draw up one or the other or revert to his original kneel.

c A variation of the basic hold in which one hand is released from *uke*'s belt to pass up beneath *uke*'s armpit and grip *uke*'s jacket on the back shoulder.

KUZURE-KAMI-SHIHO-GATAME

YOKO-SHIHO-GATAME Side four quarter hold

As with *kami-shiho-gatame* (*see* pages 106–7), the positioning of *tori*'s legs during the application of *yoko-shiho-gatame* provides a major element of the success of the technique, especially if *tori* becomes engaged in moving from one to the other as can often happen during *randori* or a contest. In general, *tori*'s legs are spreadeagled to the rear, with his hips lowered and his bodyweight flattened if *uke* attempts to bridge or twist to his far side, away from *tori*. Should *uke* attempt an inward turn, towards *tori*, then *tori* draws up both knees to wedge them firmly against the side of *uke*'s body, controlling any further movement in that direction.

Should *tori*'s flattened posture with outstretched legs not be sufficient to control *uke*'s outward turn away from him, then *tori* can usually block the escape attempt by rolling forward slightly to place the top of his head on the mat close in to *uke*'s rib cage.

Flat on his back, *uke* has both feet and legs clear by which to assist bridging or any other escape attempt. If necessary, *tori* can further control the by shifting into *kuzure-yoko-shiho-gatame* and grasping the far trouser at the thigh to take the leg out of action.

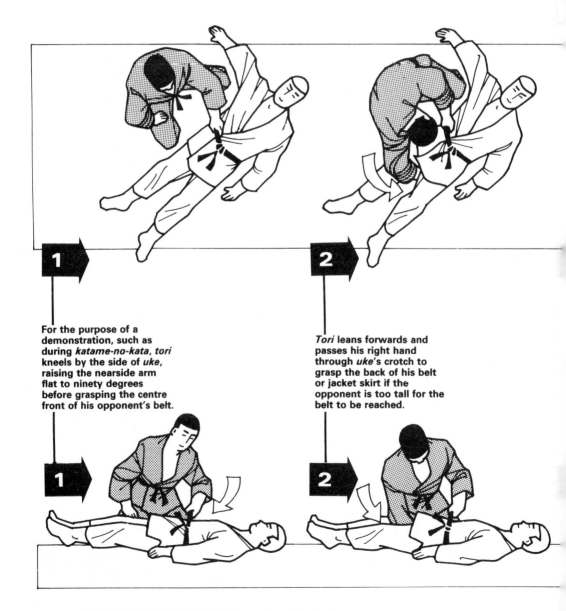

1 For the purpose of a demonstration, such as during *katame-no-kata*, *tori* kneels by the side of *uke*, raising the nearside arm flat to ninety degrees before grasping the centre front of his opponent's belt.

2 *Tori* leans forwards and passes his right hand through *uke*'s crotch to grasp the back of his belt or jacket skirt if the opponent is too tall for the belt to be reached.

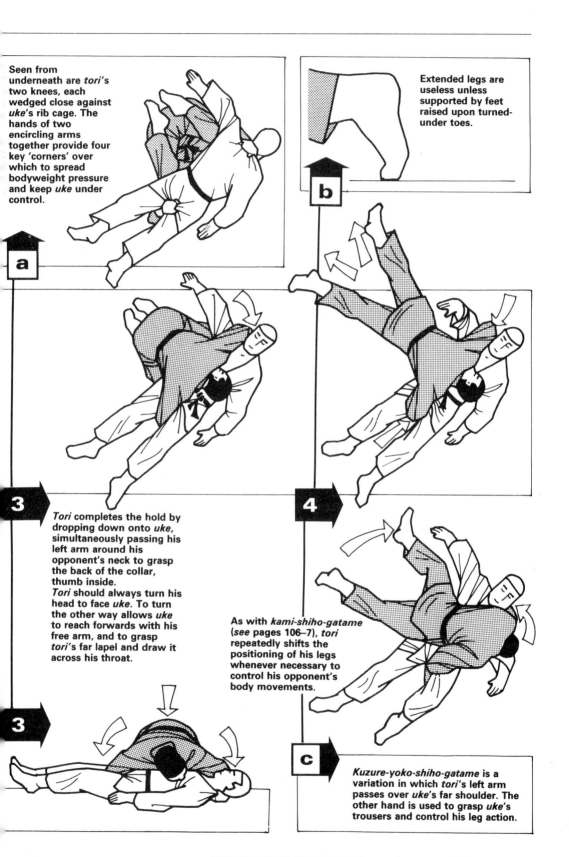

a Seen from underneath are *tori*'s two knees, each wedged close against *uke*'s rib cage. The hands of two encircling arms together provide four key 'corners' over which to spread bodyweight pressure and keep *uke* under control.

b Extended legs are useless unless supported by feet raised upon turned-under toes.

3 *Tori* completes the hold by dropping down onto *uke*, simultaneously passing his left arm around his opponent's neck to grasp the back of the collar, thumb inside.

Tori should always turn his head to face *uke*. To turn the other way allows *uke* to reach forwards with his free arm, and to grasp *tori*'s far lapel and draw it across his throat.

4 As with *kami-shiho-gatame* (*see* pages 106–7), *tori* repeatedly shifts the positioning of his legs whenever necessary to control his opponent's body movements.

c *Kuzure-yoko-shiho-gatame* is a variation in which *tori*'s left arm passes over *uke*'s far shoulder. The other hand is used to grasp *uke*'s trousers and control his leg action.

TATE-SHIHO-GATAME Trunk hold

Tate-shiho-gatame is an ideal hold-down to roll into as a follow-through to a sacrifice throw such as *tomoe-nage* (*see* pages 78–9) and then once in the basic position there are several variations to the manner in which *uke*'s arms may be secured in order to maintain control.

However, there are two potentially hazardous aspects of this technique with which *tori* should be familiar. One is the complete freedom of *uke*'s legs and feet to provide a base for a bridge-and-twist attempt at escaping. *Tori* can do little about this except keep his knees gripped tightly into *uke*'s lower rib cage, with his feet curled under *uke*'s thighs, pressing down hard to maximise his bodyweight contact.

The other danger is that if *tori* positions himself too high up on *uke*'s body, he may be easily rolled forward and over the top of his escaping opponent. Finding himself subject to this, *tori* may block the escape attempt by pressing the top of his head into the mat alongside *uke*'s head.

Hopefully, *tori* will be giving his opponent too much to worry about protecting himself from one arm lock or another to have time to think about bridging!

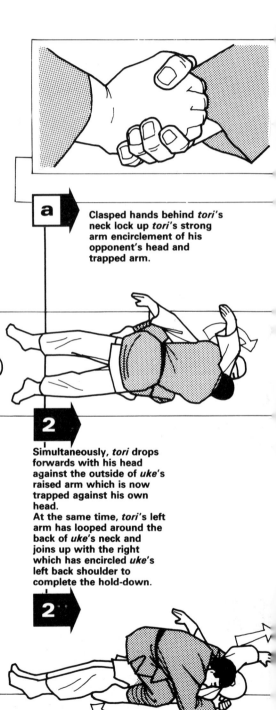

a Clasped hands behind *tori*'s neck lock up *tori*'s strong arm encirclement of his opponent's head and trapped arm.

1 *Tori* sits astride his opponent as *uke* raises his left arm and *tori* pushes it across his front towards his opponent's right shoulder.

2 Simultaneously, *tori* drops forwards with his head against the outside of *uke*'s raised arm which is now trapped against his own head.
At the same time, *tori*'s left arm has looped around the back of *uke*'s neck and joins up with the right which has encircled *uke*'s left back shoulder to complete the hold-down.

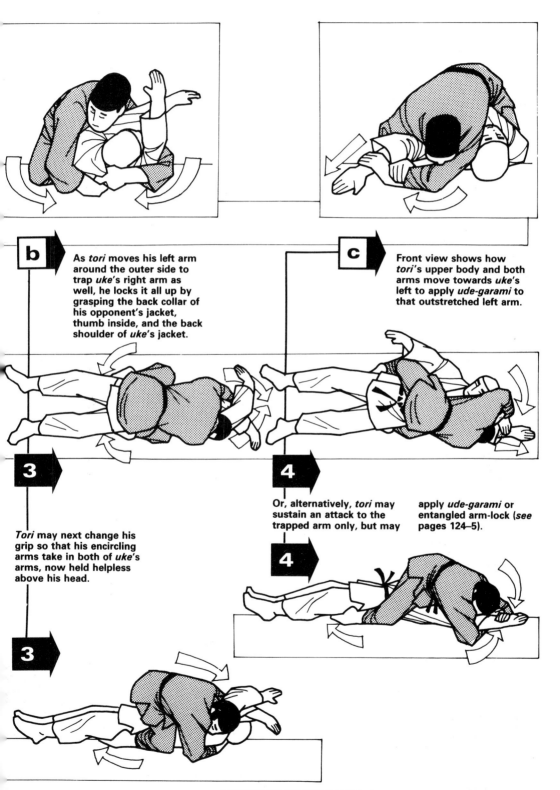

b As *tori* moves his left arm around the outer side to trap *uke*'s right arm as well, he locks it all up by grasping the back collar of his opponent's jacket, thumb inside, and the back shoulder of *uke*'s jacket.

c Front view shows how *tori*'s upper body and both arms move towards *uke*'s left to apply *ude-garami* to that outstretched left arm.

3 *Tori* may next change his grip so that his encircling arms take in both of *uke*'s arms, now held helpless above his head.

4 Or, alternatively, *tori* may sustain an attack to the trapped arm only, but may apply *ude-garami* or entangled arm-lock (*see* pages 124–5).

ABOUT SHIME-WAZA Strangle techniques

Generally classified as 'strangle techniques', *shime-waza* is a range of techniques which includes both strangles and chokes (some variations combine both). A choke, of course, is an attacking pressure across the front of the throat or windpipe, while a strangle comes about when pressure is applied to the carotid arteries at the side of the neck.

A choke is painful and may result in asphyxiation. A strangle restricts the supply of blood to the brain and can cause unconsciousness within seconds.

The effect of expert application of any *shime-waza* is so swift that there is no time for *uke* to begin working out various methods of either delaying submission for as long as possible or even trying to work out escape attempts. Such counter actions need to be well rehearsed in the *dojo* with a co-ooperative partner and, certainly to begin with, under the direction and care of a knowledgeable *sensei*.

So, until some degree of proficiency in resistance is achieved, the best advice is to tap hard in submission the moment an opponent has got a *shime-waza* working on you. At the same time, *tori* must release *uke* the very instant a tap of submission is felt or heard. On occasions, *uke* may be unable for some reason to tap against *tori*'s body and in such a case he must make repeated strikes to the mat with a flat hand or even a foot.

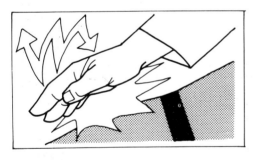

Uke must have no hesitation in tapping hard against *tori* to signify submission to a strangle or any other technique causing unbearable pain or possible injury.

Of course, the best defence against any *shime-waza* is never to get caught in one, but the possibility of that ever happening is so remote that the sooner a *sensei* teaches a beginner the skill of resistance or escape, the better for the student.

Categorised as groundwork, *shime-waza* can be applied within the rules of *judo* while contestants are standing upright, though generally they are not so instant or powerful from that posture.

GYAKU-JUJI-JIME
Reverse cross strangle

The outstanding difference between *gyaku-juji-jime* and the other two *juji-jime* techniques shown opposite is the positioning of the thumbs and fingers as the opponent's collar is grasped.

For *gyaku-juji-jime*, *tori* takes a deep grip of *uke*'s collar, with both sets of fingers on the inside and both thumbs on the outside.

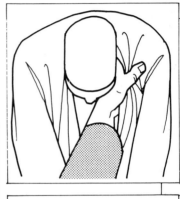

1

Tori's first hand slips deeply around the opposite side of *uke*'s neck to grip the collar, with fingers inside and thumb on the outside.

2

Tori's second hand passes across the top of the first to slide deeply around the other side of *uke*'s neck, fingers inside and thumb outside the collar.

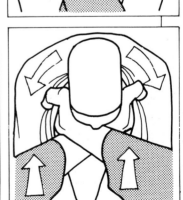

3

Tori bends both arms, with his forearm against *uke*'s throat. He twists the wrists so his knuckles press hard against the arteries.

TA-JUJI-JIME
f cross strangle

this form of *juji-jime*, the first hand to pass
ply into the opposite side of *uke*'s collar takes
rip with fingers on the inside and thumb on the
side of it. The wrist of the second hand passes
r the top of the first wrist to reach round the
er side of *uke*'s collar, taking a grip with
jers on the outside and thumb on the inside.

NAMI-JUJI-JIME
Normal cross strangle

In this third form of *juji-jime*, both of *tori*'s hands
are plunged deeply into *uke*'s collar, taking identical grips with the thumb of each inside the collar
and fingers outside. All *juji-jime* techniques are
interchangeable from one to another to suit shifting circumstances and they are highly versatile in
the postures from which they can be applied.

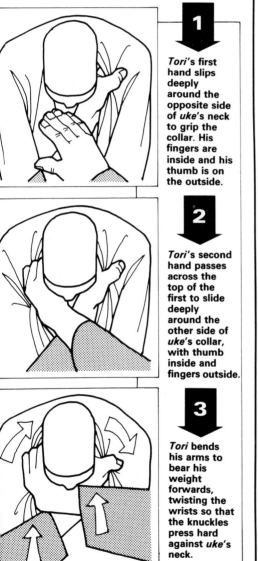

1 *Tori*'s first hand slips deeply around the opposite side of *uke*'s neck to grip the collar. His fingers are inside and his thumb is on the outside.

2 *Tori*'s second hand passes across the top of the first to slide deeply around the other side of *uke*'s collar, with thumb inside and fingers outside.

3 *Tori* bends his arms to bear his weight forwards, twisting the wrists so that the knuckles press hard against *uke*'s neck.

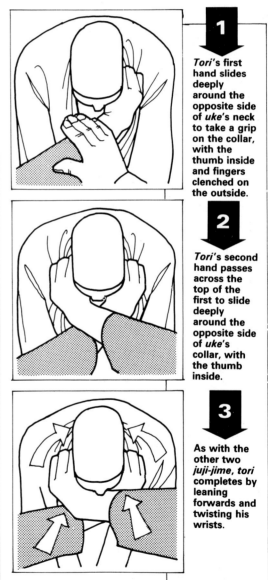

1 *Tori*'s first hand slides deeply around the opposite side of *uke*'s neck to take a grip on the collar, with the thumb inside and fingers clenched on the outside.

2 *Tori*'s second hand passes across the top of the first to slide deeply around the opposite side of *uke*'s collar, with the thumb inside.

3 As with the other two *juji-jime*, *tori* completes by leaning forwards and twisting his wrists.

TSUKI-KOMI-JIME Thrusting choke

Tsuki-komi-jime is one choke that can be a surprise attack from a standing or kneeling posture, though it is possibly more effective when applied while straddling an opponent who is beneath *tori*, face-up on the ground. That way, there is less chance of *uke* being able to turn out from the direction of the choke and much greater opportunity for *tori* to bear down with his weight through the thrusting arm.

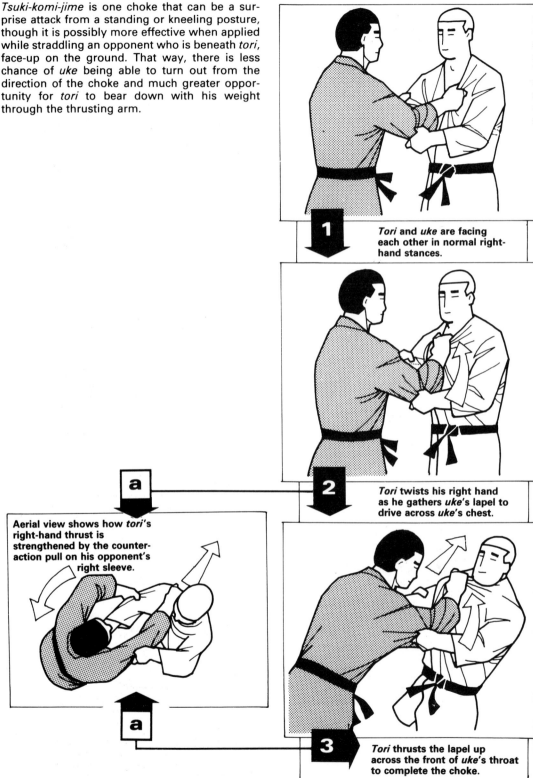

1 *Tori* and *uke* are facing each other in normal right-hand stances.

2 *Tori* twists his right hand as he gathers *uke*'s lapel to drive across *uke*'s chest.

a Aerial view shows how *tori*'s right-hand thrust is strengthened by the counter-action pull on his opponent's right sleeve.

3 *Tori* thrusts the lapel up across the front of *uke*'s throat to complete the choke.

OKURI-ERI-JIME Sliding collar strangle

A technique designed to be applied from the rear, okuri-eri-jime is one *shime-waza* which pressures both the front and side of the neck to provide the simultaneous combined effects of both a choke and a strangle.

Tori is able to increase the choking effect if necessary by leaning slightly backwards during application, or pressing his own head against the back or side of *uke*'s head to force it forwards over the choking arm.

1 *Tori* pushes close in across *uke*'s throat to take a deep grip on his opponent's collar.

2 *Tori*'s other hand slips beneath *uke*'s armpit and across his chest to far lapel.

a Either standing or in groundwork, this variation of *okuri-eri-jime* can be applied from the front.

3 As *tori* pulls hard upwards, his other hand pulls down to complete the *okuri-eri-jime*.

KATA-HA-JIME Single wing strangle

Kata-ha-jime is a choking technique applied from the rear during groundwork and is sometimes referred to as the single-wing choke.

Performed on the ground, *tori* is able to strengthen the technique by drawing his opponent backwards so that he is almost half-reclining on the lower leg of a raised knee. Like all *shime-waza* and *judo* techniques generally, practise *kata-ha-jime* to both left and right sides.

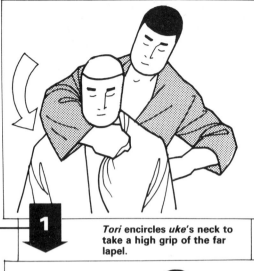

1 *Tori* encircles *uke*'s neck to take a high grip of the far lapel.

a If *uke* is on his hands and knees, *tori* may straddle his back to apply *kata-ha-jime*, but as his encircling arms come into position...

2 As *tori*'s other arm slips through *uke*'s armpit, it scoops *uke*'s arm upwards.

b ...*tori* uses a foot to push away *uke*'s supporting knee, rolling them both sideways and enabling *tori* to control *uke*'s body with encircling legs.

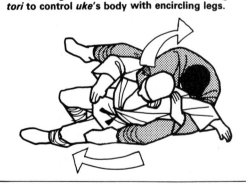

3 The technique is completed as the back fist of *tori*'s trapping arm forces *uke*'s head forwards over the forearm across the throat.

HADAKA-JIME Naked choke

This technique is referred to as the 'naked' choke because it is the bony part of the forearm which is drawn across an opponent's throat and no part of either *judoka*'s jacket is employed in making *hadaka-jime* effective.

Again, it is a technique applied from the rear and one which also becomes more effective if *tori* is able to draw his opponent close in and lean slightly backwards during its execution.

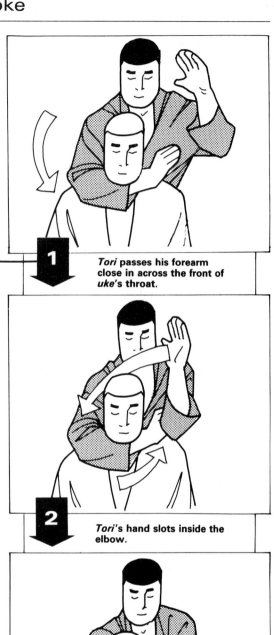

1 *Tori* passes his forearm close in across the front of *uke*'s throat.

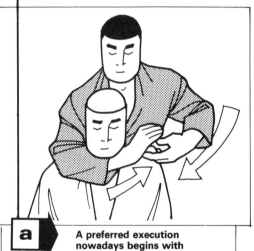

a A preferred execution nowadays begins with *tori*'s encircling arm so...

b ...hands can clasp, the arms can squeeze and *tori*'s head can apply side pressure.

2 *Tori*'s hand slots inside the elbow.

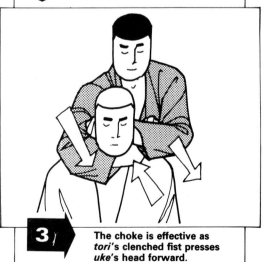

3 The choke is effective as *tori*'s clenched fist presses *uke*'s head forward.

TOMOE-JIME Circular strangle

Tomoe-jime may yield better chances of a result than other *shime-waza* when applied in a standing posture, as the application is central and *uke* has less chance of attempting an escape by turning out to either side than with, for instance, a thrusting choke (*see* page 114).

As the initial attacking movement is *tori*'s looping of the arm around *uke*'s head, it can be an opportunist technique which may come about naturally while both players are literally rolling around in search of groundwork advantage.

1 *Tori* takes *uke* off balance with a high lift-and-pull, his right elbow tipping high.

2 *Tori* pulls *uke* forwards and swivels the inside elbow behind *uke*'s head.

4 *Tori* will finally complete the manoeuvre by sliding both hands in, twisting his wrists and leaning in.

3 As his arm completes the circling movement *tori*'s other hand grasps *uke*'s far lapel.

competitive *judo*, *kansetsu-waza* is concerned only with a range of methods for applying arm-ck pressure against the elbow joint. Locks to any her parts of the body such as the legs, ankles, ees, wrists, spine, neck, shoulders, fingers and es are all prohibited.

Some *judo* associations impose age limits below hich juniors are not even taught armlocks, or angles and chokes for that matter, and they are ohibited from using them in *judo* competitions. In any case, even among mature students, the ecution of *kansetsu-waza* is an area of *judo* in hich there is a special need for care. Safety

depends very much upon an attacker's ability to control his own body strength and muscular reactions as well as those of his opponent. Just as he is exerting every ounce of muscular strength in one concentrated direction, so must he remain sensitive to a tap of submission and be able to slam immediately into reverse, switching off the power and simultaneously releasing his opponent.

If you are the defender, then as with *shime-waza* (*see* page 112) don't be shy or afraid (or stupid!) about tapping in submission too quickly.

DE-GATAME
m crush

mlocks are opportunist techniques and some ho are specialists in their application almost em to go hunting for them. Probably no other pportunity for an armlock comes more often an that presented by the proverbial straight m. Look out for it, grab it, crush it closely to you d wait for the submission which, more often an not, will follow as you apply *ude-gatame*.

1 In a simple demonstration, *tori* kneels by *uke*.

a *Uke* has attacked from between *tori*'s legs, so *tori* draws *uke*'s leading arm forwards.

b As *uke* is outstretched and falls on top, *tori* clamps both hands behind *uke*'s elbow to crush it against him for a submission.

2 *Tori* grabs with both hands behind *uke*'s elbow, drawing *uke* onto his side.

3 *Tori* completes by crushing *uke*'s arm inwards for submission.

JUJI-GATAME Cross armlock

If *kesa-gatame* (*see* pages 100–1) is generally the first hold-down technique taught to beginners, then *juji-gatame* is probably the first armlock to be learned.

The reason is, of course, that like *kesa-gatame*, it's a perfect follow-through from a throw and clearly demonstrates the importance of remaining tightly hold of *uke*'s arm throughout a throwing technique. Maintaining contact permits *tori*, within the rules of competitive *judo*, to follow into groundwork if necessary. The raised and controlled arm of *uke* presents *tori*, therefore, with the ideal posture from which to progress into *juji-gatame*.

The first move in *juji-gatame* is for *tori* to pass a foot over to the far side of *uke*'s head and it is this action which prompts some to refer to the technique as the 'step-over armlock'.

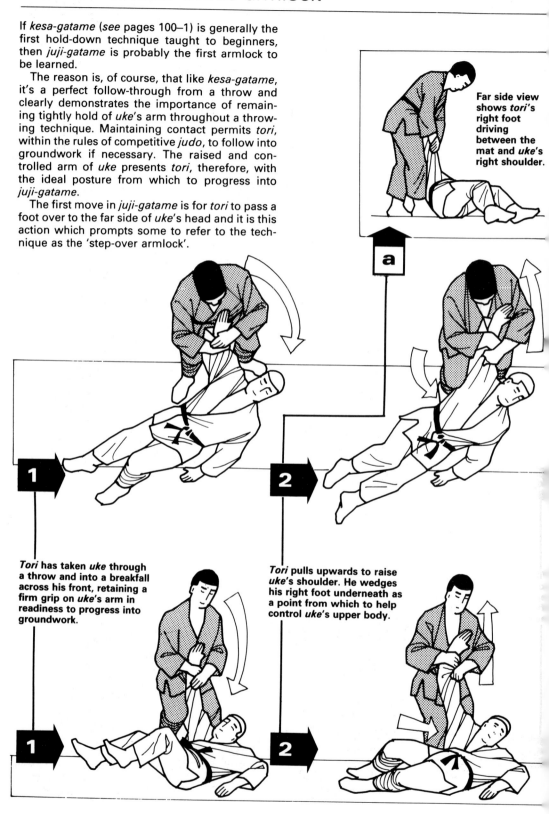

Far side view shows *tori*'s right foot driving between the mat and *uke*'s right shoulder.

a

1 *Tori* has taken *uke* through a throw and into a breakfall across his front, retaining a firm grip on *uke*'s arm in readiness to progress into groundwork.

2 *Tori* pulls upwards to raise *uke*'s shoulder. He wedges his right foot underneath as a point from which to help control *uke*'s upper body.

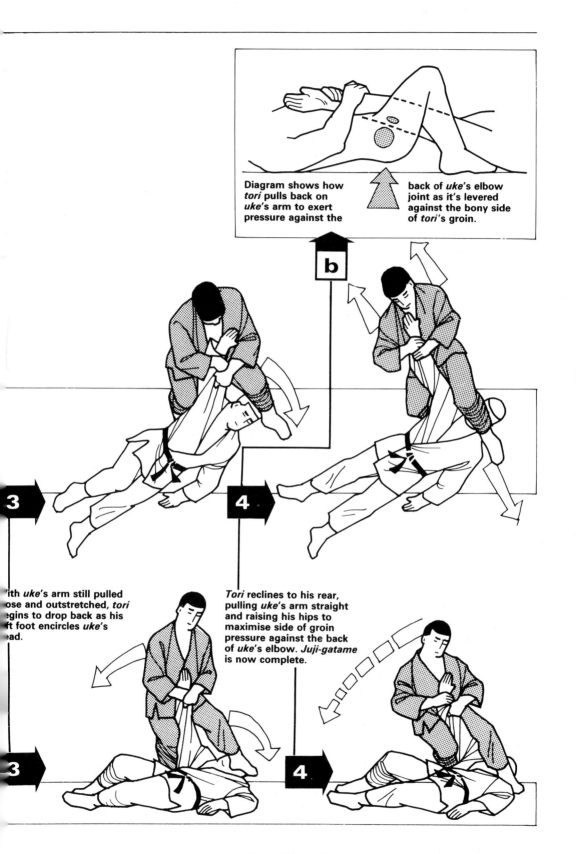

Diagram shows how *tori* pulls back on *uke*'s arm to exert pressure against the back of *uke*'s elbow joint as it's levered against the bony side of *tori*'s groin.

b

3 With *uke*'s arm still pulled [cl]ose and outstretched, *tori* [be]gins to drop back as his [lef]t foot encircles *uke*'s [he]ad.

4 *Tori* reclines to his rear, pulling *uke*'s arm straight and raising his hips to maximise side of groin pressure against the back of *uke*'s elbow. *Juji-gatame* is now complete.

3

4

HIZA-GATAME Knee armlock

Hiza-gatame can sometimes begin while both players are in standing or kneeling postures, but once thrown to the side the procedures become identical.

Several different parts of the body – hands, legs, arms and feet – are all brought into the build-up and ultimate application of *hiza-gatame*, and its appearance as a comparatively complicated technique probably puts off many from trying it during a contest situation.

However, like any other technique which may at first seem to be complicated, break down *hiza-gatame* into its individual segments, learn their postures, then link them together with a co-operative partner and practise the complete move at less than full speed to both left and right sides. Full speed of execution will come naturally.

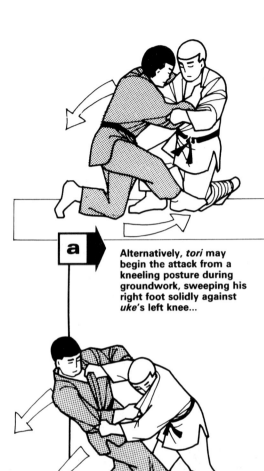

a

Alternatively, *tori* may begin the attack from a kneeling posture during groundwork, sweeping his right foot solidly against *uke*'s left knee...

1

Tori and *uke* are facing, having taken normal right-sided grips on opposite sleeves and lapels as *tori* draws *uke* forwards onto his left foot.

2

As *tori* sweeps his right leg to provide a foot pivot just below *uke*'s left knee, *uke* is drawn further forwards and off balance by the pull of *tori*'s bodyweight being thrown backwards. *Tori* falls back, twisting towards his rear right corner and using his arms to pull *uke* into a straight forward direction.

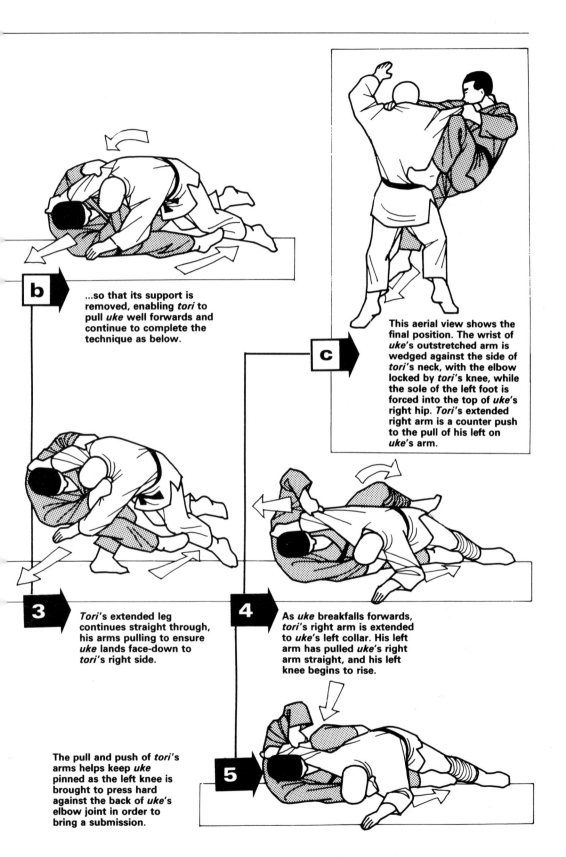

b ...so that its support is removed, enabling *tori* to pull *uke* well forwards and continue to complete the technique as below.

c This aerial view shows the final position. The wrist of *uke*'s outstretched arm is wedged against the side of *tori*'s neck, with the elbow locked by *tori*'s knee, while the sole of the left foot is forced into the top of *uke*'s right hip. *Tori*'s extended right arm is a counter push to the pull of his left on *uke*'s arm.

3 *Tori*'s extended leg continues straight through, his arms pulling to ensure *uke* lands face-down to *tori*'s right side.

4 As *uke* breakfalls forwards, *tori*'s right arm is extended to *uke*'s left collar. His left arm has pulled *uke*'s right arm straight, and his left knee begins to rise.

5 The pull and push of *tori*'s arms helps keep *uke* pinned as the left knee is brought to press hard against the back of *uke*'s elbow joint in order to bring a submission.

UDE-GARAMI Entangled armlock

This is the lock that the experienced *judoka* will slip into quite easily during the heat of a contest, yet when asked to demonstrate the technique out of context many will flinch with hesitation or ponder over what seems to be another complex grip.

An alternative name for the lock is 'the figure four': thinking of '4' is reminiscent of the shape formed by the interlocking arms when the technique is applied. This can make the lock much easier to remember on such occasions as grading examinations when the technique will have to be performed in isolation.

Once the principle is grasped, *ude-garami* can be applied from various postures with effective results. Another one to rehearse in the *dojo* with a co-operative partner!

a Should *uke* gain some advantage on the ground by rolling *tori* over, *tori* can regain authority from below by grasping a loose arm at the wrist...

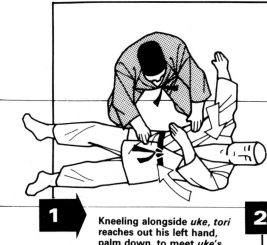

1 Kneeling alongside *uke*, *tori* reaches out his left hand, palm down, to meet *uke*'s left hand as it swings up towards him.

2 *Tori* turns his hand to grasp his palm against the underside of *uke*'s wrist so that when he leans forwards to force the arm to the mat his hand is palm down over the wrist of *uke*'s hand, which is now palm upwards.

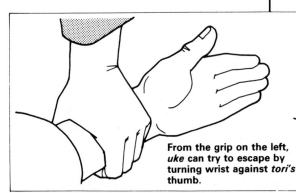

From the grip on the left, *uke* can try to escape by turning wrist against *tori*'s thumb.

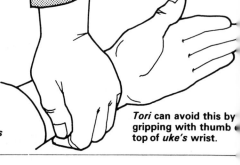

Tori can avoid this by gripping with thumb on top of *uke*'s wrist.

2 ...and threading his other arm through to grip his own wrist, form the 'figure four' and apply a variation of *ude-garami*.

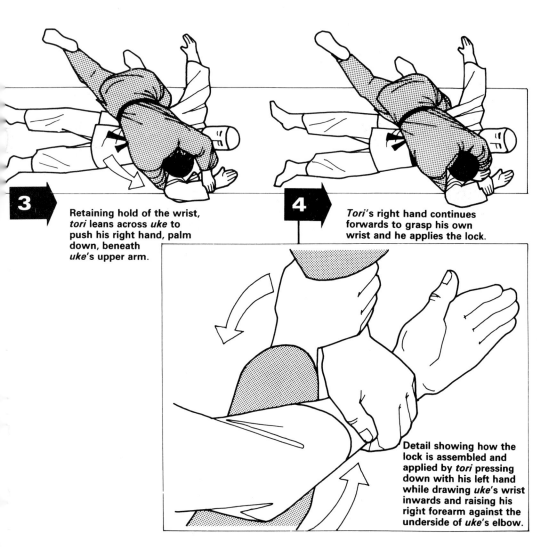

3 Retaining hold of the wrist, *tori* leans across *uke* to push his right hand, palm down, beneath *uke*'s upper arm.

4 *Tori*'s right hand continues forwards to grasp his own wrist and he applies the lock.

Detail showing how the lock is assembled and applied by *tori* pressing down with his left hand while drawing *uke*'s wrist inwards and raising his right forearm against the underside of *uke*'s elbow.

WAKI-GATAME Armpit armlock

This is another *kansetsu-waza* which can exploit an outstretched arm offered by a careless opponent and which can be applied from either a standing posture or when in various groundwork situations.

Tori's bodyweight can drop with some force as his armpit covers the back of *uke*'s elbow, especially when the move is started from a standing posture. *Tori* must therefore have practised to achieve sufficient control over his own muscular body reactions to be able to halt the action and help avoid any unnecessary injury instantly upon a tap of submission.

At the same time, *tori* must seat his armpit squarely upon the back of *uke*'s flattened elbow joint for *waki-gatame* to be effective. An armpit over the forearm is no good. An armpit over the upper arm is equally useless and, what is more, if your position it too far up you may find yourself penalised for what others might interpret to be an illegal attack against the shoulder joint.

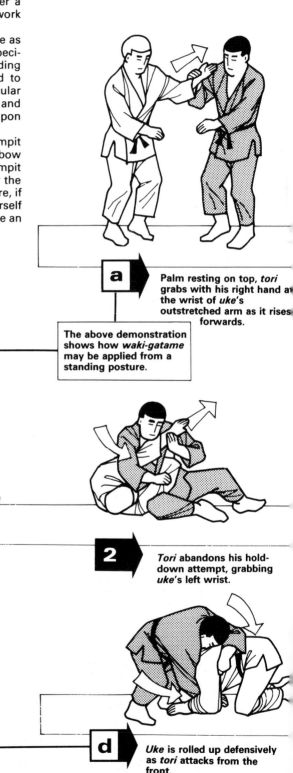

a Palm resting on top, *tori* grabs with his right hand at the wrist of *uke*'s outstretched arm as it rises forwards.

The above demonstration shows how *waki-gatame* may be applied from a standing posture.

1 *Uke* struggles to free his trapped arm to escape from *tori*'s *kuzure-kesa-gatame* hold-down and he twists to fling his left arm across the front of *tori*.

2 *Tori* abandons his hold-down attempt, grabbing *uke*'s left wrist.

Another example of the application of *waki-gatame* during groundwork.

d *Uke* is rolled up defensively as *tori* attacks from the front.

b He sidesteps to draw it across his front and steps forwards deeply with his right foot in readiness to...

c ...loop his armpit over the back of *uke*'s elbow, pulling the arm tight and straight, leaning well over it to apply full pressure and awaiting a submission.

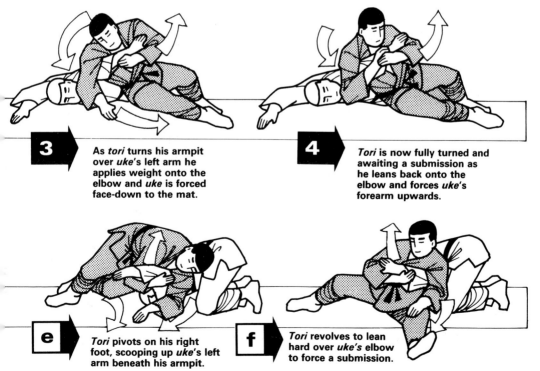

3 As *tori* turns his armpit over *uke*'s left arm he applies weight onto the elbow and *uke* is forced face-down to the mat.

4 *Tori* is now fully turned and awaiting a submission as he leans back onto the elbow and forces *uke*'s forearm upwards.

e *Tori* pivots on his right foot, scooping up *uke*'s left arm beneath his armpit.

f *Tori* revolves to lean hard over *uke*'s elbow to force a submission.

INDEX